The Best Possible Life

Copyright © 2024 by Jim Murphy.

All rights reserved.

Except as permitted under the United States Copyright Act of 1976, no part of this publication may be reproduced or distributed in any form or by any means, or stored in a database or retrieval system, without the prior written permission of the publisher.

All trademarks are trademarks of their respective owners. Rather than put a trademark symbol after every occurrence of a trademarked name, we use names in an editorial fashion only, and to the benefit of the trademark owner, with no intention of infringement of the trademark. Where such designations appear in this book, they have been printed with initial caps.

Inner Excellence is a registered trademark. Published by the Academy of Excellence - New York – Rome – Tokyo

ISBN: 978-1-7346548-4-4 (paperback)
ISBN: 978-1-7346548-5-1 (audiobook)
ISBN: 978-1-7346548-6-8 (ebook)

The contents of this book are for informational purposes only. The content is not intended to be a substitute for personal, professional psychiatric or psychological advice, diagnosis or treatment. Always seek the advice of your medical professional or other qualified mental health practitioner with any questions you may have regarding a medical condition.

Cover design by Muhammad Qaisar and Volodymyr Arabadzhy
Interior design: Irena Kalcheva

# The Best Possible Life

How to Live with Deep
Contentment, Joy, and
Confidence—No Matter What

JIM MURPHY

The Best Possible Life: to overflow with love, joy, peace, patience, kindness, goodness, faithfulness, gentleness, and self-control.

*For my sister Naomi T. Murphy
The one who taught me how to smile
and be grateful—no matter what.
See you soon.*

My Lord God,

I have no idea where I am going.
I do not see the road ahead of me.
I cannot know for certain where it will end.

nor do I really know myself,
and the fact that I think I am following your will
does not mean that I am actually doing so.

But I believe that the desire to please you
does in fact please you. And I hope I have that desire
in all that I am doing.

I hope that I will never do anything apart from that desire.
And I know that if I do this you will lead me by the right road,
though I may know nothing about it.

Therefore will I trust you always though
I may seem to be lost and in the shadow of death.

I will not fear, for you are ever with me,
and you will never leave me to face my perils alone.

— Thomas Merton, Trappist Monk

Contents

Introduction	1
My story	3
Part I: Your Story	**11**
1. The Great Need	12
2. The Two Extreme Challenges	20
3. The Ultimate Dream	26
4. The Great News	34
5. The Three Worlds	37
6. The Double Deceptions	45
7. The Beginning of the End	51
8. The End of Religion (as we know it)	59
Part II: Amazing Awaits	**65**
9. How to Get the Best Possible Life	66
10. How to Think About the Best Possible Life	73
11. How to Live the Best Possible Life	79
12. How to Train Your Heart	91
13. How to Let Go of Your Attachments	105
14. How to Live in the Flow of Resonance	113
15. How to Pray	121
16. How to Know if You're Doing God's Will	132
Conclusion	144
PS.	150
Index	**152**
FAQs	152
Where to Go From Here	160
Acknowledgments	164
Notes	166
Glossary	176

Introduction

The word vocation comes from the Latin vocare, to call, and means the work a man is called to by God. There are all different kinds of voices calling you to all different kinds of work, and the problem is to find out which is the voice of God rather than of society... The place God calls you to is the place where your deep gladness and the world's deep hunger meet.

— Frederick Buechner

In May 2023 I went on a boat trip with a couple friends. We sailed away from civilization for a few weeks and had time to examine our lives—without the noise and busyness and prime deliveries that so easily distract us from the beauty and grace of a simple life, lived on purpose.

We got to experience solitude—that place where fear meets hope and a decision needs to be made. In this tension-filled space, we must consider who we are, the path we're on, and what's possible in our lives. Of course you can skip over the decision—to be courageous or not, to face your fears or not—and jump to the next task, the closest distraction... and avoid the call of your heart, the one that's longing for depth and meaning and fullness of life. But you know at some point, of course, a solitary moment will find you again.

On the days we were anchored, there was always excitement for what adventure awaited. For me, the great adventure was to sit in that floating office and dream big dreams, to imagine possibilities, and see what, at the end of the day, the God of the starry universe might reveal to me.

It was on one of those days that I felt called to share my deep gladness with what's now more than ever, the world's deep hunger.

Since the Covid-19 pandemic of 2020, the world has become a different place. It's a 24/7 world bursting with busyness and anxiety—and very little community. It's a world filled with fear, dissention, and isolation. There's a deep hunger for connection—real heart-to-heart, meaningful relationship, with the kind of love that's fearless and forever.

You were created for that kind of relationship, the out-of-this-world kind where the love is unconditional and fully reliable. It's your deepest need—to be loved so powerfully by someone so solid and stable that you can rest secure, with the deepest contentment, joy, and confidence—no matter what.

In the busyness and stresses and comparisons we face, it's easy to lose sight of what's possible, of the life you were created for.

This book is about that life that awaits. It's about a love you can feel in your heart that enlivens every experience, everything you think, feel, and do. It's about having courage, facing fears, and acting on your longing for depth and meaning and fullness of life. It's your calling. *The Best. Possible. Life.*

My story

On April 1, 1991, I took off my Chicago Cubs uniform for the last time. My dynamic vision had somehow left me—important for hitting a 90 mile-an-hour baseball—and my minor league career was over. The cheering was done. So was the love and acceptance. It was April Fool's day but this was no joke.

Nineteen years later, I found myself sitting on the curb in sunny and cold Denver, Colorado with my mind racing and nowhere to go. Just like that day, nineteen years earlier, it felt like my life was over. Except this time, it was much worse.

It was February, 2010 and I had spent my life savings and was $90,000 in debt. My credit cards were maxed out and I had no money in the bank. I moved to the desert to live in solitude, to confront my fears and hopes and dreams. I wanted to make sure that when it came to the end of my life, that I had fully lived.

I ended up spending 50-60 hours a week doing writing and research for a book, for five years straight (two and a half years in the Arizona desert), ironically, about how to have peace and confidence under pressure. And now the pressure was caving in on me. We were in the middle of a recession and on that day in Denver, I couldn't see a future. My knees were shaking and my mind was spinning out of control. I had an I-could-fall-to-the-ground sort of anxiety; the trip to the mental hospital kind.

I thought, *"You've put all your eggs in one basket. Sure the book (Inner Excellence) is in bookstores around the world, but you've got no money to hire someone to market the book, you don't know how to do marketing, and you don't like to promote yourself. If no one hears about the book, no one will buy the book, and if no one buys the book, the bookstores will pull it off their shelves, and you'll be a total failure and everyone will know it. And of course no pro athlete will hire a failure to coach them... So you'll have to get a regular job, but in this recession, nobody's gonna hire a failure. Not the corner mini-market, not 7-Eleven, nobody. You're gonna die alone in the streets."*

Looking back I can see what happens when you isolate yourself and one negative thought leads to another (even if they're absurd), with no one to question the voice in your head, no one to assure you that you're ok.

When my knees started to shake in Denver, I called my friend Ricky Scruggs and asked him what to do. He said, "Find a homeless person and help him." Right around the corner a homeless person was playing a full-sized harp for donations. (You know how those harpists seem to be everywhere.) I looked in my wallet and I must have taken a cash advance from one of my maxed-out credit cards, because there was $100 in there. I gave it to him.

I went back to where I was staying to run on the treadmill, hoping to clear my mind. After the run I returned downtown and found a Starbucks coffee shop and place to sit. I stared into the abyss, just trying to make it through the day. Then the homeless harpist walked in.

He walked past me, stopped in his tracks, then turned around and said, "Are you the guy that gave me that money?" I said yes.

He thanked me and left, only to return with a card, a bracelet he made, and a box of chocolates. He gave all three to me.

Before I go on, there's a detail you should know. When I was writing *Inner Excellence*, I asked my friend Jennifer if she could take a look at it and make sure it lined up with the Bible. She read the manuscript and asked me, "Have you heard of the word Zoe? It's mentioned in the Bible many times. Zoe is the Greek word for life—absolute fullness of life; to be filled with vitality. I think that's what your book is about," she said.

"Yes! I replied. "My whole life I've chased success and numbers and status, when what I've always really wanted was to feel fully alive."

So I began to orient the book around the idea of pursuing absolute fullness of life and letting everything else be added to you. Rather than focusing on developing external skills to be successful, I discovered a profound idea: if you develop the person first—their inner world—their skills will be maximized in every area and their entire life will transform.

In the Starbucks on that long, anxiety-filled day, I opened the homeless harpist's card. It read,

Thank you so much for caring for me.

Love,
Zoe

My heart skipped a beat.
"Your name is Zoe??" I asked.
"Yes," he nodded.

I asked him if he knew what his name meant. He said no. I told him it means absolute fullness of life and I just spent five years writing a book about it. I signed a book for him and never saw him again.

That was the beginning of the most extraordinary, transformational, miraculous year of my life. When I think of my life, I think of pre-Zoe and post-Zoe. Before that mind-spinning, anxiety-filled day in Starbucks, and after.

A few weeks after meeting Zoe I had another extraordinary experience. I was in North Vancouver, B.C. and a stranger I just met began telling me about my life. He said, "You're a coach aren't you? You're banging your head against the wall because you have all these goals but you're not getting anywhere." I was thinking, *Yes, you're exactly right, but how do you know this about me?*

After a while a gal named Jamie, who I also didn't know, walked over and handed me a picture of a kite she had just drawn.

"What's wrong with this picture?" she asked.

"Your kite doesn't have a string," I replied.

"That's right. That kite is you. You're like a kite without a string; a slight breeze would blow you away," she said. Incredibly, that's exactly how I felt. I was so weak emotionally—lost and adrift. The weight of the world was on my shoulders. I had a million things to do and no idea how to do them. My life felt helpless and hopeless.

These two strangers seemed to know all about me at a time in my life when it felt like no one did. They prayed for me and my life began to change. It was April 1, 2010, April Fool's Day, nineteen years to the day after I hung up my Cubs uniform for good.

They invited me to a bible study that night and I felt God telling me, *"There's nothing you've ever done or could ever do that would change how much I love you."* The feeling in my heart transformed from the heaviness of a Mack truck to the lightness of a gentle breeze.

That night, I said a short, heartfelt prayer:

God, I give you my life. I don't care what you do with it, I just want your peace. I surrender my life to you. If you want me to give up coaching and all my possessions, move to Nepal and volunteer in an orphanage the rest of my life, I'll do it. I don't care what it is, just tell me what to do.

That simple prayer changed the direction of my life. It marked the beginning of a slow but steady journey towards recovery: getting back on my feet, gaining inner strength, and most importantly, embracing a whole new way of living. I gave God control of my life and started learning to hear his voice and let him lead the way. No more self-reliance (well... much less anyway).

In the next year and a half, I had more unexpected, amazing experiences, with more strangers telling me what God told them to share with me. The most memorable message-from-God-through-a-stranger moment came in the summer of 2011. I was at my friend Tarun's house in North Vancouver, about to leave, when his mother called on video from India.

"Tell your mom I said hello," I said walking out the door.

"Hey Jim, my mom's friend wants to talk to you," he replied.

So, I sat in front of the laptop and heard words I'll never forget. This lady thousands of miles away whom I had never met said,

"God wanted me to tell you a few things... Everything you've been going through has been training for you. God's going to bring people from all over the world to work with you. He's going to bless you, it's going to happen soon, and you're going to know it's from God."

Very specific words about my life and how it was about to change.

A few weeks later, early in the morning, I was half awake when I heard a voice say, "Jim, are you ready? Things are going to happen fast."

I said, "Yes, God, I'm ready." Before I finished that sentence my alarm went off. I thought, *Hmm, maybe he's serious.*

Several weeks later I was contacted by Jude O'Reilly, a golf caddie in Dublin, Ireland, who worked for a Swedish professional golfer named Henrik Stenson. He said, "I just read *Inner Excellence*, can you talk to my boss? He could really use your help." So, I flew to Sweden in the Fall of 2011 and started to work with Stenson.

Several weeks later I got a call from Tiger Woods' coach, Sean Foley. He read *Inner Excellence* and asked if I could meet with him and his client, Hunter Mahan, who had been struggling. So, I flew to California and met with them, and started to work with Mahan.

A couple weeks later I received a call from David Novak, the CEO of YUM Brands (Taco Bell, KFC, and Pizza Hut). He said he read *Inner Excellence* and would like to work together. Novak also sent the book to some of his executives in Europe and I started to work with them as well.

I flew to Geneva, Switzerland and led an *Inner Excellence* offsite retreat for the leaders of KFC Germany, Spain, Netherlands, and a handful of others. We shared an incredible time together, discussing *Inner Excellence* principles and clarifying the vision for their lives. We're still friends to this day.

A few months after we began working together, Mahan won a PGA Tour event, and then he won the World Championship (Match Play) a few months after that. Stenson also turned things around and in 2013 went on to win the FedEx Cup (PGA Tour end of season championship).

I've been coaching professional athletes and executives around the world ever since (as well as leading *Inner Excellence* retreats), and now I get to share the source of everything good in my life, what I've learned and how I learned it, with you.

This book, *The Best Possible Life*, shares with you how to connect directly with the source of love, wisdom, and courage, and live with *absolute fullness of life*. You'll learn how to become your true self, the one in sync with the flow of resonance, grounded and connected to the creator of the universe. You'll see how that one decision to surrender my life to God completely changed my life for the better in every way, and how it can do the same for you. *The Best Possible Life* is about who God is and therefore who you are, what he's doing in the world and how you can join in.

Thanks for joining me on this incredible journey.
Love Jim

PART I

Your Story

The Great Need

The day Chris Baldwin arrived at Lake Youngs Elementary was a normal day for everyone, except two of us: Chris and I. Chris arrived in the middle of the school year and he was the new kid. I was the fastest kid (well, in my grade anyway). So that meant one thing: new kid had to race fastest kid to see if there was a new fastest kid.

At Lake Youngs, being fast and athletic was a very desirable attribute. Winning the race with Chris would be quite significant: Perhaps I would get the love and acceptance I desperately craved. Like most humans, my entire life has been one long journey wanting you to love me, to say how great I am, to introduce me as, "This is Jim. He's smart and fast and he's done this and that," and other various *you-should-be-impressed*-type phrases that bring raised eyebrows of adoration. My win on the playground years ago meant I could still feel good about myself. That's kind of how life is, isn't it? We think the next achievement or status will get us the love and acceptance we desperately desire.

My life has been punctuated by moments where I've received the love I've craved, and so many where I haven't. The missed moments of love and acceptance created a filter over my eyes that narrowed my vision, seeing more of what I've missed than what I've been given. It's formed an armor of self-protection, where I've been triggered by reflections of rejection and memories of mistakes that translated into uncaptured opportunities, or worse.

The thing is, I'm human, which means I have a subconscious mind designed to protect me, so, it remembers the wounds I've received to guard against future ones. I also have a heart that longs for love and an ego that wants to be praised and adored. Most of all, I've got a deep need for something this world cannot fill, and I've unknowingly spent most of my life searching for ways to fill it. All my fruitless efforts have created a fear of rejection that's been hard to shake.

This... is my problem.

This... is every human's problem.

In grade school I was smart and fast, but it was never enough to give me love that was unconditional. It was *always* conditional, dependent on how fast I ran or the grades I got or the popularity I gained (or failed to gain). I was constantly trying to get you to think well of me, so I could feel good about myself.

This self-consciousness continued into adulthood, and so when you speak, I think about how it impacts my life—or doesn't, and why would you tell me then? I've always thought about *my* goals, *my* dreams, *my* fears, *my* family, *my* self. I want to be a good guy, I do, but most of my life has really been about my needs and desires and people who've lined up with those needs and desires (bingo) and those who haven't (sayonara).

I'm not saying this is good or I liked it, I'm saying I've gotten caught up in self-absorption, endlessly trying to improve my life with better results and circumstances, so I'll feel better about myself and so you'll respect me, even though it's a never-ending treadmill.

The truth is, all my striving has been an effort to feel accepted and secure, so I can stop comparing and feel so loved that I can finally, fully rest.

That sort of love and rest is what we're created for, that our hearts beat for. Without it, we spend far too much time consumed by the three major symptoms of a compulsive, harried life: over-thinking, negative thinking, and self-conscious thinking (concern for what others think).

Take myself, for example. I've thought way too much about my life and what I want but can't control, and how I don't know how to fix things in my life and I don't know what you think of me or if you like this book or if perhaps after reading this sentence you'll throw the book across the room and it will poke someone in the eye and they'll be maimed for life and you'll tell them it was my fault and I'll feel bad and maybe because of it I'll never write another book and at least that way I'd never write a sentence again that was so long and self-centered, and at least you could rest knowing you would never waste another minute of your life with this garbage and you could live a peaceful life with your dog and your life would be so much less violent.

It's exhausting.

What about you? Have you ever overanalyzed things, perhaps about what other people think? Have you ever gotten caught up in negative, self-conscious thinking? Have you ever felt that something's missing, that all your striving has only delivered temporary happiness, surface-level satisfaction?

THE GREAT NEED

Something *is* missing. It's the non-judgmental, ever-expanding vision of beauty and joy that's available to all of us, when we get out of our own way, when we let go of our petty quibbles and offenses taken, when we accept the love and connections that are meant to fill us with meaning and amazing moments. Our own minds confine us and we miss so much.

Our minds become a lens that sees the world through all the rejections and mistakes we've made. It's fed our ego's fears and increased the need to be liked and get likes.

We all live in our own worlds, the ones we've imagined. The truth is, I don't see the world as *it* is, I see the world as *I* am. You don't see the world as it is, you see the world you've built in your mind, story by story, and now it's 100 stories high.

The world you see is a reflection of your inner world and the story you've been telling yourself with all the memories, mistakes, and melodramas that have become your life. It can be scary navigating a story with so many tall tales and countless disappointments and failures crowding the rear-view mirror.

When all our pursuits—even the successes—bring only fleeting fulfilment and ultimately return empty, we don't know what to do. So we do the opposite of what we should—we get more consumed with ourselves and our stories. This, of course, only magnifies the problem.

The self-in-the-center lens through which we see the world is distorted, reflective, and immensely biased. What we see is the result of the ever-changing filter that has interpreted all the experiences we've ever had. For example, when I walk into Starbucks, I only see what impacts my life, and what I see first (perhaps subconsciously), are potential threats and then possible mates and then probable waits in line that I really don't have time for.

The problem is, you and I, and all the other humans, are born with a nature that's been infected. The biggest challenge we face, in performance and in life, is fear. **At the root of fear is a virus of the heart: self-centeredness.**

Self-centeredness, in our discussion, is a natural preoccupation with self that limits our vision and stunts our growth. It's putting yourself in the center of the world and seeing everything from how it impacts you, your family, your work, your life. It's like being a baton in the conductor's hand of the most amazing orchestra in the world and the whole time thinking you're an incredible dancer with flawless rhythm. The self-in-the-center life becomes a dark filter of pride that limits your vision and stunts your growth.

Perhaps you think you're not self-centered, certainly not as oblivious as a baton in the conductor's hand, thinking you're the center of attention. However, consider this: is not everything you think, say, and do based on your experiences, your goals, and your beliefs? When you've gotten upset, was it not generally something that was yours that was threatened?

The problem of self-centeredness is that it imparts an inaccurate view of the world, where *you're* the subject of the story, the one who succeeds or fails and makes his or her own decisions. The subject of a story, as you may recall from grade school, is the central idea or theme around which the story revolves. It's totally natural (and logical) to view yourself as the subject of your life story and of course to have a sense of pride about it (this is a good thing, right?) The truth is, however, that you're part of a much larger story—a story you're in, but that's not *about* you.

Making your life story about yourself is like a honeybee that doesn't realize it's part of a colony with a daily guided mission, or a branch that doesn't realize it's part of a vine. Your life is one part of a larger life, just like your hand is one part of your body. You need the arms, legs, heart, and all the parts, to be whole.

The heart is the control center of the human, in charge of disbursing life throughout the body. The lifeblood reverberating through humans is love—the red essence of mortality. **We're made whole through love—an interconnectedness with God and others that we cannot, sustainably, live without.**

If you don't know how you're connected and nourished and filled with life, you'll constantly be searching, disconnecting, and isolating yourself. You may end up feeling like a kite without a string, where the wind is whipping and wild.

To see yourself as the subject of your life story is the fundamental human error. It's a mindset that hijacks our hearts and leaves us continually scrambling to build walls and systems and gather achievements and possessions so we can be secure. But we never get secure that way—especially when we stop to think of all the things that are out of our control and all the dangers and possible perils that we can never do enough to mitigate.

Living this self-as-the-subject life puts us on a path of compulsive busyness trying to do what we cannot. We're trying to fit in and stabilize ourselves in an unstable world obsessed with achievement and appearances... constantly trying to appear in everyone's feed when what we desperately need is to be fed ourselves—the real food, real drink, and real nourishment that can only come from unconditional love and connection.

We become zombies, driving in our metal coffins, going to jobs we don't love so we can buy things we don't need, in order to compare well with others who are doing the exact same thing.

We have this deep need for unconditional love and acceptance, and since it's a chase-your-tail-endless-treadmill-pursuit that never delivers, we end up driving ourselves crazy trying to figure out how to be the person that says the right thing and has the right connections and accomplishments. This creates a cognitive mishmash that messes with our psyche and we lose track of who we are or should be.

100 years ago, American sociologist Charles Cooley described the human condition like this: *I'm not who I think I am; I'm not who you think I am; I am who I think you think I am.*

In other words, the person I present to the world is based on who I think you think I am, or should be. It goes like this: I imagine how I appear to you and everyone else, then I picture what you think of me and how you might judge me based on how I've presented myself, and then I act in response to that perception.

What Cooley shared with us is that we're all deeply connected. How we see those connections defines who we think we are and impacts everything we do. Our entire lives flow out of our interconnectedness. We live in a network of connections that starts with God and flows into people and work and the environment. It all impacts our thoughts and feelings and how we see the world.

Talking Heads lead singer David Byrne described our interdependence this way:

> *There's a sense that you're making these decisions about your life or what you want to do or say and that they're all coming from you. But they're not! Who you are at any given moment is defined by the social context. We're not quite ants, but we're social animals. To pull one ant away and say, 'That ant decided to do that!' No. We do things because we're part of a larger community.*

The truth is, you were created to have deep, meaningful relationships, and even more, for glory. Glory (as you'll see in the glossary), is the brilliance and beauty of infinite, inherent worth. A life of glory is one that has no comparison, filled with fullness of life. This sort of glory, this sort of life, is a profoundly interconnected one—with God, others, yourself, and nature, and especially, your work.

In this deeply connected community, unconditional love is the common bond, and from love comes joy. Joy is a deep sense of well-being, freedom and gratitude, independent of circumstances; it's harmony, excitement, and resonance that surpasses understanding.

The deepest need of the human heart is for the unremitting connectedness of unconditional love; and even more, for the glory that shines so bright, no darkness could ever put it out. If you don't realize your immense need for God and others to live the life you were created for, you'll take the world on yourself, which is a disconnected-tossed-in-the-wind existence. It's like living in solitary confinement when you're meant for so much more.

The Two Extreme Challenges

The world is broken and remains that way, in spite of our efforts to help it. This is beautiful, in a way, because it breaks us of our self-dependency. In a world that refuses to be healed, we must face the fact that we are not the heroes of our stories. It teaches us to rely on something bigger than ourselves and teaches the source of true compassion.
– J. Goins

In our self-absorbed lives, human life can be defined by two extreme and irresolvable challenges:

1. The extreme challenge of living in a broken world.

2. The extreme challenge of navigating a broken world that you cannot fix, especially without the deep love and connection you were created for.

THE TWO EXTREME CHALLENGES

Over time, these two major adversities are an incredible gift if they help you slow down and think deeply about the meaning and purpose of your life. Then, with God's grace, you may realize one crucial thing: *You were created for more than anything the world can offer.*

The truth is, you're going to die—you and everyone close to you. One by one, you'll see them face the ultimate truth of life on earth. And before it gets to be your turn, I hope and pray you'll stop long enough to think deeply for yourself about these words you're about to read.

No matter who you are or how much success or money, friends or followers you have, every night, when the lights go out, it's just you and your creator, alone in the dark. In that darkness, if you think deep enough, you'll realize your immense inadequacy and insufficiency and the utter lack of meaning in the world. Our inability to fix the broken things in the world, especially the fear and division, and the broken things in our own lives, creates a sense of despair, if we're really paying attention.

Many of us never think about this, because deep down, we don't want to. It's too scary. Thus many of us never realize our lack of deep connection and contentment. Instead, we keep ourselves very busy and very distracted.

It's only by busyness or distraction, often by great things like meaningful work or meditation, social connections or success, that we can forget the void that begs to be filled. American philosopher Henry David Thoreau said, "Those destined for greatness must first walk alone in the desert." Often it takes separation and solitude for extended periods of time to fully face our fears and emptiness.

One of the greatest challenges we have is too many thoughts, from too many concerns, about too many things. In our anxious minds we must stay busy, because busyness keeps us from facing our deepest needs that we don't know how to fix.

The life you were created for is a life that goes well past the distractions of wealth and sex and temporary pleasures that too often sidetrack us. You were designed to live filled with the deepest need of the human heart: unconditional love and acceptance. As humans we're born with a deep desire to be fully known and fully loved, especially by someone of great significance. Unconditional love, not tied to achievement, allows you to fully relax, let down your guard, and stop trying to be someone the world can love.

Most people, perhaps unknowingly, spend their entire lives trying to earn that love.

Think about your own life for a moment. What goals have you set and why do you want to accomplish them? Isn't it because you think (and hope) they will bring you great satisfaction, a real sense of achievement so you can feel good about yourself and have a sense of security no matter what the future holds?

What if you spend your whole life chasing your dream but never achieve it? Or perhaps worse, what if, with countless hours of sacrifice, you do achieve it, but the payoff turns out to be temporary, empty, and meaningless?

The problem is that once you achieve your dream (if you ever do), your heart still doesn't have what it needs most. And it's not like you can rest on that achievement. Once you achieve great success, more people will expect more things from you—and you may not be able to deliver. The expectations never end.

It's a broken world filled with broken people—all trying to do enough to be enough, but it's never enough. Some folks may come across as well put together, highly educated, and ultra-accomplished, but each of them has wounds and fears and the same deep need for love and acceptance that we all have.

THE TWO EXTREME CHALLENGES

We're all striving to be the person that's loved and accepted, favored and followed. The problem is that everyone's too busy with their own issues to really see each other. So, we spend our lives competing for affection, trying to build ourselves up so we'll be seen as lovable, but we're constantly rejected (often by people we don't know), and so we push harder. This turns into a constant back and forth feeling of being inflated or deflated, depending on our current situation and results and how we feel about it. Or, perhaps more accurately, how we feel others feel about it.

We're all in desperate need of nourishment for our souls, a lifeline of unconditional love that doesn't depend on what we say or do, what we have or achieve. It's just that that's not something the world offers. It's like trying to guess a five-letter word in six attempts or less—and not being allowed to use vowels. You'll never get it with those restrictions. We're continually trying to be real and yet we're being really inauthentic. We're living artificially un-intelligent, trying to navigate an Instagram-BeReal-please-see-me-social-comparison world where everyone's trying to find love without the heart to do it.

As hard as we try on our own, we may get brief bouts of happiness, tiny tastes of wonderment, but our deepest desires continue to go unmet. This is because we're born with a heart that longs for glory, for unhinged joy, in a world that can't deliver. If we don't find it in our work, we'll try to find it in possessions or status or a person. But there's no work or status, no possession or person that will meet your soul's greatest desire. Every person is human, and every human is broken.

Everyone but one, that is. The one who created the earth and came down to look us in the eyes and invite us to love him with the love that He gives us, the everlasting kind. *This* is your invitation.

It's an invitation to fill the deepest need of your heart: unconditional love. Like a clock without batteries, you'll always have an emptiness in your heart until you choose to accept the love of the one who created you for a relationship with him. Accepting God's love changes everything in your life: it gives you a deeper connection to yourself, to others, to your work, and to nature. No matter how much time goes by, nothing will ever change at your core until you connect to the source of power for which you were created.

Everybody worships

"In the day-to-day trenches of adult life, there is actually no such thing as atheism. There is no such thing as not worshipping. Everybody worships. The only choice we get is what to worship.

And an outstanding reason for choosing some sort of God or spiritual-type thing to worship — be it J.C. or Allah, be it Yahweh or the Wiccan mother-goddess or the Four Noble Truths or some infrangible set of ethical principles — is that pretty much anything else you worship will eat you alive. If you worship money and things — if they are where you tap real meaning in life — then you will never have enough. Never feel you have enough. It's the truth.

Worship your own body and beauty and sexual allure and you will always feel ugly, and when time and age start showing, you will die a million deaths before they finally plant you. On one level, we all know this stuff already — it's been codified as myths, proverbs, clichés, bromides, epigrams, parables: the skeleton of every great story.

The trick is keeping the truth up-front in daily consciousness. Worship power—you will feel weak and afraid, and you will need ever more power over others to keep the fear at bay. Worship your intellect, being seen as smart—you will end up feeling stupid, a fraud, always on the verge of being found out. And so on."

– David Foster Wallace, *This is Water,*
2005 Kenyon College Commencement Address

The Ultimate Dream

In order to discover the character of people we have only to observe what they love.

— St. Augustine

What's your ultimate dream? What if you could have a ten-million-dollar house on the water, completely paid off, and have all the normal cares and concerns of the person who owned that house? Would you take it? Of course you would. On the other hand... would you rather live in an apartment, paycheck-to-paycheck, for the rest of your life, with no savings, but... be guaranteed deep contentment, joy, and confidence, every day until you die?

For myself, most of my life I wouldn't hesitate—I'd take the house in a heartbeat. Of course, there's no right or wrong answer to this question, just a way to consider what's in your heart, and what it beats for.

Say, like me, you chose the house. Perhaps it would bring you many amazing experiences and great parties, and you'd feel so loved. But, maybe it wouldn't.

To help with your decision, consider this: What if no one could ever see your beautiful house besides you? And what if no one could even know you had it—would you still choose it? Isn't the reason you want that beautiful home so you can have people over and have these great get-togethers where everyone loves you and is so grateful for you, so you could feel... deep contentment, joy, and confidence? If that's so, why not go directly for what you want most?

Most of us spend our lives pursuing an illusion, striving for some seemingly great thing that we think will make us happy. Instead however, our version of success, even if we get it, often leaves us empty, like a house that's not a home. What if you found out that pursuing the wholehearted life you were created for gives you the best chance to have what you deeply want, including a gorgeous home?

What you'll find, as you continue to read, is that what takes the most space in your heart—what you worship—determines everything else about you. We all worship; the question is who or what you worship. We all want an amazing life with the freedom to do what we want. But what is that life? More specifically, what's the best possible life for you and how do you get it?

I've always wanted to live The Best Possible Life; the only thing that's changed is how I define it. When I was younger, I thought the best life was one where I was hitting home runs and making millions of dollars. I wanted to be the person that I thought every girl would love and every guy would dream of being.

What I've since learned, however, is that what I've always really wanted is to feel fully alive. I just figured that was the way to do it. I thought that if I could set myself up with really good life circumstances by getting really great results, I could have an amazing life. I envisioned that life being one with incredible experiences, captured through a combination of great friends, great situations, and perhaps some great challenges. Maybe it would be hitting a home run to win the World Series and having a big house on the water that people raved about. Then, I figured, I would feel really good about myself, and hopefully, feel really good when I'm *with* myself, and my thoughts.

Now I've come to realize that absolute fullness of life is completely independent of circumstances. You can have the most amazing moments in the most mundane settings, or the most anxiety-riddled or depression-filled feelings amidst the world's most glorious ocean views. So, it's not the situation or circumstance. It's not the result or success or trophy. It's what's in your heart—and when *what* you love with all your heart is the most empowering thing in the universe, well, then fullness of life becomes *your* life.

Thus, part of living The Best Possible Life is to learn what to love and what to let go of. It's learning to have the right structure and the proper boundaries—around your thoughts, desires, and loves—that will bring fullness of life.

For most of us, our feelings and desires have been running our lives. We have limited ability to resist desires, especially around social media and work. We struggle to stop working or checking our phones because we fear we might fall behind or miss out.

According to a study by Hofmann, et al (University of Chicago, 2012), the average adult spends approximately eight hours per day feeling desires, three hours resisting them, and half an hour yielding to previously resisted ones. In other words, we spend a lot of time and energy managing our feelings and desires and we're not great at directing them to empowering ones. What the authors of the study found is that self-control is more about building good habits so they'll replace bad ones rather than using willpower.

The most powerful way to create good habits is to elevate our desires. We need to know what's best for us so we can love it the most. You can start by figuring out what you've been chasing so far. What's the real reason you've been doing what you do? What's the bottom line? Perhaps the most common desire when I speak with someone about what they want most is freedom.

Freedom is awesome, but what does having freedom actually mean? You might think that freedom means having the most options, but too many choices often causes anxiety. The American fast-food chain *In-and-Out Burger*, for example, showed us that *fewer* options often creates more excitement and a better experience than a restaurant with countless options. Not only does too many choices often cause anxiety, it misses the point of freedom itself.

What most of us long for when we think of freedom is deeper and broader than having multiple options to craft happy moments. We want to feel connected to a vision, secure in who we are, engaged in something that makes us feel alive. We want a deep sense of well-being that creates an inner lightness, a buoyancy that keeps us spirited in our mission, thriving in our purpose. True freedom allows us to live free from self-protection and social comparison, inspired by and devoted to a vision beyond ourselves.

This sort of freedom allows us to reject disempowering desires and embrace empowering ones. For this to happen, we need to live according to our true design, with the proper restrictions and environment. If you "free" a fish from water and put it on the grass, it loses the constraints and limitations it needs to live a full life (or any life). We're like the fish—certain restrictions are necessary for us to live an extraordinary life. We can't just indulge in all our impulses, giving in to every pleasure or desire. That would dissipate our energy and scatter our resources. Our life force needs to be directed down a path that's powerful and permanent.

So, we need to reject some desires and embrace others. We need to let go of our attachment to what we want but can't control. Besides, you have your plans and goals, but how often are your desires actually what's best for you? When you realize that you don't know what's best for you (circumstance-wise), then you can begin to walk in love, not fear, and stop clinging to what you want but can't control.

The clinging part is the problem. We cling to what we want because we feel our identity and security is riding on it. We've placed our foundation and sense of self into something unstable. When we come to the unsteady moments in life, we think about our desires and fears and how we can't control the outcome. We think, "Who will I be if I fail, lose my job, or get rejected?"

When we cling to this narrow view of our lives, we don't take the risks we need to live bigger, fuller lives. "In order to hit the best shot of your life, you need to be willing to hit the worst," says Teddy Scott, PGA Tour caddie to world #1 golfer Scottie Scheffler. To be your best in golf or baseball, wrestling or writing a novel, you need the freedom to fail.

Most people spend their entire lives pursuing temporary satisfaction and fleeting feelings of happiness because they're trying to navigate a broken world without the proper resources. Their lives get consumed with chasing success or money or numbers—running after the wind—even though they're created for so much more. They're all over the place because they're not sure what will last and what will pass.

The one thing that lasts, that determines everything you think, say, and do, is your heart. Your heart is where inner peace and inner strength, joy and self-control, all fade or flourish. Your heart is where your greatest dreams and biggest fears are. Get those two opposites (your dreams and fears) in your heart to join forces, structured within the boundaries of your true self, and you'll have the freedom to live with fullness of life.

In short, your heart is the key to everything you want—in this life and the next. Here's something that may help:

Your heart needs a great devotion, something deeply meaningful to attach to, otherwise it will grab on to the next closest thing, which is personal happiness.

The pursuit of happiness leads us to try to control what we cannot (continuously trying to get good circumstances so we can get good feelings) as well as trying to protect what we have. It's a life of self-protection that leads to fear. To get out of this fast track to fear is to have a heart that sees beyond the self, a heart connected to what's powerful and permanent.

Since the human default is self-centeredness, our hearts need training. Heart-focused training is the most important thing you'll ever do. By training your heart, I mean training it to pursue what's most empowering, to love most what's best for you, so you can drop the barriers of self-protection and self-absorption.

It's similar to training your appetite to love eating what's best for you. You don't need to train yourself to love carrot cake or chocolate chip cookies; it's easy to want those things. The training you need is the training to choose the broccoli and brussels sprouts, to not go just by taste but by long-term effects. It's the same with your heart. You don't need to train it to love comfort or pleasure; you need to train it to love what's going to have the most beneficial impact on your life, no matter how difficult or painful.

And this does require training, because a naturally self-centered heart won't train on its own. We have egos that see the world through a filter of self-protection and self-enhancement. Our hearts and egos don't see actual reality or truth; we see *our* reality and *our* truth. That kind of seeing can be severely limiting. (Note: When I say ego, I mean that part of your mind that's always comparing, always threatened, and never satisfied).

As humans, we're easily deceived by our hearts. We're told to follow our hearts—and that can be a great thing—but not if your heart is in the default mode (divided), leading you on a self-centered journey towards fear.

What if you felt with all your heart that you need to try fentanyl, or smoke pot to make yourself happy, or have unprotected sex with someone you just met? You'd feel it as true—but it would be wrong. At any given time, your heart may be 100% leading you toward a life of pain and misery—which is why your heart needs training.

Anglican pastor Dr. John Yates III explains:

> *There's a trend in the adoration of authenticity: 'You be you. Follow your heart (even if it lacks awareness of others). I am who I am. Keeping it real. I refuse to fake it. I'm just being authentic...*

There's just one problem with this, as Dr. Yates continues:

> *The human heart is corrupt, deceptive, and self-destructive... When we pursue every passing affection in an attempt to satisfy the longing of our hearts, we rocket down the road of self-destruction.*

Your identity—your true self—is to have a heart that's filled with sacrificial, unconditional love, a love that doesn't come from you or anyone else in this world. It comes from a single source—the creator of the universe—and there's an endless supply. With this kind of love, you're free to dream great dreams, to pursue uncharted waters.

To be your true self is to let go of your past failures and inadequate desires (the ones that dissipated your energy and joy) and align your truth with capital-R Reality and capital-T Truth. For this to happen, we need to cast off all that's held us back.

To live the ultimate dream is to let go of our limited desires and the stories we've created about ourselves. You'll need to ask yourself some hard questions that perhaps you've don't want to ask or haven't wanted to face.

- Are you willing to let go of who you've been to become someone you've never been before?

- Are you willing to face feelings you've never faced before?

- Are you willing to sit in the discomfort, keeping the walls of protection down (the ones that isolate you), and learn to get comfortable being uncomfortable?

It's hard, maybe the hardest thing you've ever done—but it's worth it. Because the Reality is, the story of your life is far greater than you've ever imagined.

The Great News

You were created for an extraordinary life, the best possible one. It's a life of amazing experiences with deep, enriching relationships, a life where you're continually learning and growing, making a difference in the world. You were born to experience absolute fullness of life (in Greek: zoe), to do great things and feel fully alive.

No matter who you are or what you've done (or even plan to do), this life is waiting for you. Once you realize your deep need, if you search for this life with all your heart, you'll find it. The fact that you're even reading this is because God is reaching out to you. He's been reaching out to you since before you were born, yearning to hold you in his infinitely secure arms.

The capital-T-Truth is that God created you for an extraordinary purpose, and it's never too late to discover what that is. **It doesn't matter if you're a drug addict, a convicted killer, or both**. That's part of the wonderful news. Your entire life can be one where at every turn you've returned evil for good, endlessly cursing God and rejecting him in every way possible. It doesn't matter. You might think you're too old or you've made too many poor life choices, but the reality is there's nothing you've ever done or could ever do that would change how much God loves you. (While there are things that can separate you from his love—of your own choosing—we can discuss that later).

The greatest gift you could ever receive is wisdom, wisdom to realize your deep need—and the instability and void in your heart—so you can humbly receive a life far beyond your dreams.

Wisdom is to know who God is and therefore who you are, what he's doing in the world and how you can join in.

You were created by God and for God—in his image—to have a personal, direct relationship with him. When I say a personal relationship with God, I mean having the same access to him that a toddler has to their parents. It's like Tim Keller said, "The only person who dares wake up a king at 3am for a glass of water is a child. We have that kind of access." That's the kind of access you were created for, except this king never sleeps.

The one who spins the earth, grows the grass, and calls each star by name, watches you sleep every night. He sees your chest rise and fall with every breath you take, with the loving tenderness of a mother to a child.

The life you were created for is not about a distant God who doesn't care about your day-to-day life. It's quite the opposite. Just like a mother wants her child to be happy, God truly wants you to be happy—he delights in every detail of your life. But he wants so much more for you than just your happiness. He wants to be your best friend—forever...to be the one who sits on the floor with you and laughs and cries with you.

He didn't create you to have an ordinary life. He created you for glory, for a life immeasurably more valuable and empowering than the fame of Hollywood or having millions of followers. God created you to have an incredibly deep, enriching relationship with him. He also created you to do amazing things—too many to list—*which he prepared in advance for you to do.* He wants to fill you with unlimited peace, joy, and confidence... to realize your infinite, inherent worth. To live fully. Forever.

The Three Worlds

In the 1999 movie *The Matrix*, a software developer named Thomas Anderson is offered a choice: swallow a pill and learn the truth about the world (that it's all a fabrication—a virtual reality)... or swallow a different pill that lets him continue on with his boring (and unaware) life, believing whatever he wants to believe.

We're like Thomas. We live in a world that isn't what it seems. We're immersed in a culture that's chosen the second pill, going about our daily lives as if we're living in reality, as if what we see with our eyes is all there is.

There's actually much more going on than the eyes can see and ears can hear. Like Thomas, you have a choice. You can continue on with your busy life and the same goals and heartbreaks, fears and anxieties. Or, you can stop clinging to a life that's less than what you were designed for.

Like a sunflower to the sun, you can surrender to God's unlimited power and embrace both the sunshine and the rain. You can let go of your efforts to weather the storm by improving your circumstances, and instead, let him transform *you* in the midst of it.

If you stop for a second and look at the people around you, perhaps you'll glimpse what life in Western culture has become. We're like little white rabbits hurriedly scurrying about, going from task to task, consuming transactions like carrots. In our busyness we get emotionally attached to our goals and things we think we need. In doing so we miss so much. In chasing our pursuits that provide only fleeting moments of pleasure or happiness, we miss out on a world of lasting abundance.

Here's a guide to help you think about this. I call it the *Three Worlds Model*.

When you're born, you enter into three worlds:

World 3: The transactional, consumeristic culture you're immersed in, with all your results and consequences. It's the world all around you that you can see, touch, taste, smell, and feel.

World 2: Your inner world of words and thoughts, feelings and decisions—and the actions that come from those thoughts and feelings.

World 1: The invisible world of love, wisdom, and courage. The world that has ultimate control over the one you can see, touch, and feel. A world of unlimited possibilities—limited only by imagination and belief.

Let's take a closer look at each world:

Third world[1]

The third world is the culture we live in 24/7, the one with tangible results and circumstances. It's the world of success or failure, win or lose, profit or loss—the bottom line of all your efforts. It's how we're evaluated, whether it's your grade point average or batting average, birdies or bogeys, strikeouts or home runs. It's the outcome of all the work you've put in. It's a binary world of situations and consequences that make us happy or sad and thus are "good" or "bad." There's bills that need to be paid, scores that need to be counted and wins and losses attributed. It's a temporary, transactional, zero-sum world that's constantly luring us with shiny rewards and tempting treats, but so often leaves us empty.

World three is the world of expectations and evaluations, comparisons and consumerism. While there's many great things in this third world that we live in (amazing people and companies, hospitals and orphanages, for example), it's also unstable, unfair, and very fleeting.

The third world is the world of the past and future and the one in which you have the least control. Every goal you ever set, and every result you ever get, are all in the past and future. It's a world of scarcity and instant gratification; a finite world where you're continually evaluated and always on trial. It's where ego and fear abound.

---

[1] The term "Third World" arose during the cold war to define countries not aligned with either NATO or the Warsaw Pact. Many of these countries were economically poor and undeveloped. This term is no longer used. Now the proper term is developing countries.

Second World

The second world is your inner world and the actions you take each moment, based on your thoughts, feelings, and decisions. Think of world two as the workings of your mind and heart, and the actions that you take based on those inner workings.

Here's how it unfolds:

- You take in (3rd world) information through your senses (you see, hear, touch, taste, or smell something).
- This produces a thought.
- Your thought brings a feeling.
- Your feeling causes you to act.

This is a simplification of course. The heart and subconscious take in all the incoming information from your senses and filters it through your beliefs, all of which may happen in a split-second. And since we all have our own unique (biased and filtered) lens through which we see the world, two people may see, hear, touch, smell, or taste the same thing, and have completely different experiences.

So, world two is how you live, work and perform, based on the processes in your heart and mind. It's the world of your nine-to-five, your daily life and performance, where you make moment-to-moment choices—the world in which everything hinges.

First World

The first world is the world of unlimited love, joy, and peace, wisdom, courage, and confidence. Like the sun that never stops shining (sometimes hidden above the storm clouds), these resources are always there, forever waiting for you. That's because they're attributes of God himself, who never changes and has loved you from the beginning.

The first world is the spiritual world where there's an unlimited supply of inner strength and inner peace, mental toughness, beauty, and every good thing. It's the connectedness of your true self, where your heart belongs—the reality of heaven.

The first world is the unseen, intangible, eternal world where every good thing originates. It's the world that constantly whispers wisdom to those who slow down and truly listen—to those who seek God with all their heart.

How it works

Every day when you get up, your heart wants to connect to the first world and your ego looks immediately to the third world. Your heart (at least part of it) longs for things that last forever like love, joy, and peace. Your ego capitalizes on your greatest need, which is the need for unconditional love. Because you're created to love and be loved, the ego always tries to convince you that the next promotion, connection, or success will get you that love. Then you can fit in. Then you can be ok.

Thus, the ego is always on the lookout, continually pushing you for more and better ways to measure up. The only problem is—and it's a big one—is that the ego is never satisfied. It's eternally empty and begging for more, always inflated or deflated. You're always being vetted. The ego puts you (and everyone else) on trial every day, continually evaluating what people are thinking and how you're doing. The problem is that it's not a fair courtroom. No matter what the jury decides, you'll still be on trial in the next moment, and the next, and the next.

For most of us, our entire lives have been third-world-based (3-2-1 worlds oriented), looking at our circumstances and results to see how we're doing and thus how we should feel about ourselves. That would be like a pilot trusting only what she sees through the windshield and rear-view mirror and not using the instrument panel. The eyes are important, but they're secondary. The control center (first world) is key. If the pilot is only using her limited vision, she's missing most of the information that's sustaining and directing the airplane.

The third world—what you can see with your eyes—is a temporary world and the one in which we have the least control. You can do everything right, be the most worthy employee, teammate, or spouse, but if the boss or coach doesn't choose you, or your spouse no longer wants you, it doesn't matter how things appear or how qualified you are.

When we wake up and immediately check our phones, look at emails and scroll through social media, we're starting our days in reaction mode, based on what the world says we should focus on. This type of life is a constant put-out-the-fires-emotional-rollercoaster-ride-of-emotions response to dopamine hits, luring us into an ever-increasing, superficial, surface-level existence.

The greatest lives ever lived, however, began their days in world one. Their worldly focus was prioritized 1-2-3, and stayed that way throughout the day. These people, ordinary radicals like Loren Cunningham, George Muller, or Elisabeth Elliot, lived spirit-led, purpose-driven lives. They focused on a purpose beyond their own needs and wants. They walked by faith, not by sight. They woke up every day first-world-oriented, affirming their purpose, inspired by their mission. They committed their lives to seeking first the kingdom, power, and glory that created the universe... orienting their lives around the energy that holds the stars in the sky and the oceans in place.

How about you? How do you start your day? Rather than checking your phone, what if you were to check your purpose? Rather than reacting to the news, what if you responded to God's love?

In order to live a life of deep contentment, joy, and confidence, starting your day first-world-focused is crucial. You might start by listening to music that connects you to your purpose, fueling your soul with words and energy that brings fullness of life.

Three Worlds Summary

The first world is your true self—your heart created in God's image—connected to the infinite resources of love, peace, and joy. The second world is you living and working/performing (your inner world and the actions that follow). The third world is your life circumstances and results.

We can think of the third world as the broken world we live in, the one we can see, touch, and feel. It's a temporary, transactional culture that we're all immersed in, where self is the center. All the good things (great companies, people, and pursuits) get elevated to higher-than-God status, the be-all-end-all, where our hearts come to love most what's transient and superficial.

The first and third worlds have the power to mold our desires and transform our hearts. The second world is where choices are made that determine the course of your life.

The first world is the Kingdom of God, where his nature flows into everything, where love creates joy and joy leads to every other good thing, starting with peace, then patience, kindness, goodness, faithfulness, gentleness, and self-control. It's the unseen, intangible world of infinite, eternal resources created for your empowerment and enjoyment.

The second world is where refinement takes place, where every day you choose how you will live. Are you going to be led around by the illusion of what your eyes see and body feels? Or will you trust and believe in the first world, the realities of heaven that you were created for but cannot see?

As you learn to let faith and Truth guide you, you'll encounter an abundant life you've yet to imagine.

In our third world culture, it's so easy to start your day dominated by your ego and get trapped in a life where you're just reacting, never creating—a slave to circumstance. Or you can build something that lasts, your true self. To drop your guard and surrender control can be a tough pill to swallow, but it's beyond the best supplement; it's the vitamin that awakens every cell in your body to the life you were created for.

The Double Deceptions

Man cannot live without joy; therefore, when he is deprived of true spiritual joys it is necessary to become addicted to carnal pleasures.
— Thomas Aquinas

The great mistake in life is to chase happiness, that elusive quest for good feelings that continually ends up with a chase-your-tail-for-good-circumstances emptiness that never delivers anything that lasts. Sure, everyone wants to be happy. We all want to feel good. There's never a time I would choose getting poked in the eye over sitting in a hot tub. However, we're created for much more than positive, temporary feelings based on what's happening. Happiness is quite possibly the lowest bar you can set, and chasing it is exasperating.

Joy, that deep sense of well-being, freedom, and gratitude, independent of results and circumstances, now that's something worth pursuing.

The main difference between happiness and joy is that one is temporary and based on ever-changing circumstances and one is eternal, the by-product of love. The pursuit of happiness easily turns into a series of karmic "try-to-be-a-good-person-so-you-can-get-good-things-in-return" transactions.

The thinking is that if I do the right thing or treat people well or do good deeds, I should get good things in return, which would make me happy. Sometimes, however, we do the right thing and we get hurt, and after this happens a few times, somewhere along the line we think, "What's the point?"

What happens is that we make mistakes in our thinking, or perhaps more accurately, we get deceived. There's two deceptions to be particularly aware of:

1. Thinking that happiness is what you really want—so you spend your life pursuing comfort and good circumstances (for you and your family).

2. Believing that if I'm a good person I shouldn't suffer—especially if I become a Christian.

They're both a trap. They're both forms of self-absorption that becomes a downward spiral of judgment and negativity, leading to despair and self-rejection. The truth is, no happy moment will last and no amount of good deeds will fix a dysfunctional world filled with pain and suffering. We're broken people living in a broken world.

We've been conditioned to think that life is about comfort and happiness and getting our desires met, when the truth is that those three things are often the biggest obstacles to living the best possible life.

When we spend our lives pursuing happiness, for ourselves and our kids, we're chasing after the wind. That's a grave mistake, because we're created for so much more—to live with peace and joy and confidence, far beyond good but temporary feelings. We're going to suffer, but we can have joy and sadness at the same time. Try doing that with happiness; it doesn't work.

When our lives are consumed with the pursuit of happiness and avoiding discomfort, a whole series of dysfunctions take place. Vision narrows, all the possibilities of the universe get pushed aside for temporary pleasures, learning stops, and fear increases.

The great deception is that I should be happy, and if I give my life to God, he should not let me suffer. The idea is that if I'm a decent person, I deserve to be happy—especially if I trust God with my life. We'll get into this more later, but when sin entered the world suffering came with it. The rain falls on the rich and the poor, the good and evil. It's a broken world and you're going to suffer—becoming a Christian doesn't change that; even if you devote your whole life to serving God and never miss a prayer or devotion. Throughout history Christians have suffered, especially Christ. Should you be any different?

When you do suffer, and you've surrendered the course of your life to God, you know you're not alone. You know that God's got you and he's working all things for your good. He also knows what you're going through—he's suffered as well. On top of that, his suffering was all *for* you, so after you go through the temporary suffering of this world, you'll enter eternal paradise.

The mindset that "If I'm good I deserve to be happy," leads to becoming judgmental, because I'm not always good but I always want to be happy. When painful situations arise, I feel sad, guilty, or ashamed, wondering if I screwed up or karma was getting me. So I compare myself to others to try and feel better.

This comparison becomes judgment, where I divide people into groups, separating them by status based on my interpretation of their worthiness or contribution to society (or lack of).

Comparison and judgment becomes a guilt-based, finger pointing, divisional hierarchy, still prevalent today, 2,000 years after Jesus came to teach us a new way—a much, much better way.

That way is to surrender your limited strength for God's unlimited power—to get out of your own way and into his way. The challenge is that it's so scary to do so because rarely do we know exactly what God is up to. So often what looks like disaster can be the best thing for us, and what looks like victory may be the worst thing for us.

Perhaps this will be helpful:

You were created for glory, but to share in the glory you must share in the suffering.

You were created for far more than happiness. You're designed for an extraordinary life, but here's what trips most people up: They don't realize that the design inherent in the best possible life has one foot in joy and one foot in suffering. It's how the universe works.

To get stronger physically, our muscles need to be broken down. To get stronger mentally, emotionally, and spiritually, we need to go through difficulty. We need to suffer. Note: I'm not talking about abuse, I'm talking about the fundamental law of the universe:

We need hardship to grow and ultimate growth comes from death—the death of your live-for-myself life.

Suffering does for us what nothing else can. It removes the pride of self-righteousness and self-reliance and allows us to move towards the foundation of wisdom: humility.

Throughout history, the ones God used the most—the ones who did miracles and lived extraordinary lives—were not the competent ones, not the smart or skilled or strong-willed. Rather, it's quite the opposite.

It's the ones who recognized they had little or nothing to offer and so they relied on God's strength and words and direction, not theirs. It's like writing a book about the most important topic in the world when you know you aren't the most qualified person to do it. You wonder at what point your readers will think, "Hey, this joker's got no Ivy credentials, and he's way out of his League, and I don't see a P, h, or D." And then you pray that God doesn't change after 2,000 years and stop using those who are weak and unqualified.

Ironically, the greatest human strength is to recognize your weakness. Using your own ability to run your life is like having a two-year-old teach physics while Einstein watches—maybe not the best use of resources.

The great news is that your value is based on what God did for you, not what you do or what the world thinks. It's a completely priceless, no charge entry into the most extraordinary life possible, one far beyond your imagination, because it doesn't come from this world.

The Malady of Desire

"The gods had given me almost everything. But I let myself be lured into long spells of senseless and sensual ease. I amused myself with being a flâneur, a dandy, a man of fashion. I surrounded myself with the smaller natures and the meaner minds. I became the spendthrift of my own genius, and to waste an eternal youth gave me a curious joy. Tired of being on the heights, I deliberately went to the depths in the search for new sensation. What the paradox was to me in the sphere of thought, perversity became to me in the sphere of passion. Desire, at the end, was a malady, or a madness, or both. I grew careless of the lives of others. I took pleasure where it pleased me, and passed on. I forgot that every little action of the common day makes or unmakes character, and that therefore what one has done in the secret chamber one has some day to cry aloud on the housetop. I ceased to be lord over myself. I was no longer the captain of my soul, and did not know it. I allowed pleasure to dominate me. I ended in horrible disgrace. There is only one thing for me now, absolute humility."

— Oscar Wilde, *De Profundis*

The Beginning of the End

The opposite of love is not hate, it's indifference.
The opposite of art is not ugliness, it's indifference.
The opposite of faith is not heresy, it's indifference.
And the opposite of life is not death, it's indifference.
— Elie Wiesel, Holocaust survivor

You were created by God, for God, for an out-of-this-world relationship with God. In the original first world (after heaven), there was the Garden of Eden, a paradise of perfection, with unlimited abundance in every way. There was joy in work, in connection to God and each other, and to the land. Then man, in his own free will, chose self-reliance and broke the connection. Evil entered the world and brought with it pain and suffering, division and desperation.

Humans became independent, separate from God and each other. In our independence and separation, we grew more and more self-oriented, which increased our need to compare ourselves with others to try and feel better. Comparison, however, is a precursor for envy and jealousy. So, in order to feel better, we've become more self-indulgent.

In our preoccupation with pleasure and our own lives, we distance ourselves from God, which dissipates our energy and, ironically, steals our joy. The more we give in to desires for instant gratification, the more it takes to feel good. Like a drug addict, we slide down the slippery slope of disconnection into disillusionment and despair.

Imagine going to the greatest restaurant in the world. Having a love for food, you're super excited. Once you arrive, perhaps in Barcelona (or maybe Copenhagen or Lima), you settle in for the best culinary experience the world can offer. When the food comes, you savor it. It dances on your tongue and lights up your senses like never before. Then what happens when you go home and eat at other restaurants? You'll constantly be comparing, yet nothing will ever compare. You'll always remember your experience at *Disfrutar* (or perhaps at *Alchemist* or *Central*).

That's how it is with our hearts. We're born with a glimpse of God's glory in the deepest recesses of our being. Then we spend the rest of our lives searching the (third) world to complete that glory, except we only find lesser things that never compare. Although we're designed to be fed and nourished with the best sustenance in the world, we continually settle for less. And when we sustain ourselves with lesser fuel, it takes more and more to satisfy less and less. Thus, we become prone to addiction.

We've all been addicted to something. The third world has stolen our hearts. Maybe it's pleasure or security or comfort. Perhaps it's social media (and the fear of missing out) or success. What's been your addiction? What's been your go-to when life gets hard and you're scared and anxious? What have you dreamed about or feared about in your spare moments?

The bible shares a story of two cities (Sodom and Gomorrah) whose citizens continually gave in to their lesser desires. They went their own way, disconnected from the Truth and the unfolding story of God's love for us. They allowed themselves every pleasure that sex and money could obtain. Instant gratification and reckless self-indulgence became the norm, forgetting God and each other. Pleasure was their god and they ignored those in need. Both cities disintegrated in a fiery death.

You might think that the unbridled lust and pleasure-filled parties were the primary offences against God (and each other), but those were just the by-products. The root of their self-centeredness occurred in four areas. They were:

1. Arrogant.
2. Overfed.
3. Unconcerned.
4. Unhelpful toward the poor and needy.

In other words, they were *indifferent*. Life revolved around their own needs and desires and they lacked concern for others. The scary thing is that it's a deceptively gradual slide. It starts with self-confidence.

We accomplish some task or get the result we want, so we feel good about ourselves. We gain confidence and start to think we're the source of our success, so we become self-reliant.

Self-reliance, that crucial part of life that we learn as we enter adolescence, becomes self-protection and self-promotion. These are helpful things that can help you get good grades, a good job, and many other good things. But they're only temporarily good, like diapers on a baby, or training wheels on a bicycle. Soon they need to come off or you'll never become the person you were meant to become. You'll spend your entire life striving (with your own strength) to gain things, to be successful. Perhaps you will be, but you'll always have to stay busy to avoid the emptiness inside. You'll put up walls to enhance your life, but instead they'll imprison it. You'll always be afraid of losing what you have. You may gain the whole world but lose your soul.

Self-confidence easily leads to self-reliance or self-rejection. When we're confident, if it goes well we become self-reliant. If it goes poorly, we gain anxiety and feel bad about ourselves. Either way, we try harder to be successful no matter how it went, increasing self-reliance.

When we're self-reliant as well as naturally self-centered, it's easy to lose sight of the truth. When the truth is hazy, our abilities and limits also become unclear. It's what some call the Dunning-Kruger effect.

In 1999 two Cornell psychologists tested participants on logic, grammar, and sense of humor. They asked the ones who scored in the bottom quarter to rate their skills. Surprisingly, they ranked their skills as far above average. Their lack of knowledge caused them to overestimate their own abilities. Not only did they score in the bottom quartile, but their self-in-the-center lives robbed them of the awareness to realize it.

Interestingly, the same thing happens with what's possible in our lives.

We underestimate our future because we don't know what we don't know. So we get comfortable living lives of quiet desperation, playing small, building walls, isolating ourselves from the truth of our great need, as well as the greatness that awaits those who believe.

To summarize, self-confidence—so important as a youngster—becomes the very thing that can keep us from seeing the truth about who we are and what's possible in our lives. Confidence is great and it's one of the things professional athletes want the most, but self-confidence has drawbacks as well. It can create carelessness and pride (self-inflation) that gives us an inaccurate view of the world, and when we fail, it can turn into self-rejection.

The problem with self-confidence

I was talking to a Major League Baseball All-Star pitcher recently at an *Inner Excellence* retreat. We were discussing confidence and he said he doesn't spend much energy on confidence. "I've felt confident and performed badly. I've felt low confidence and performed great. Confidence in general hasn't had a big effect. *I felt the less confident I was the more present I would have to be,*" he shared.

In other words, being present was more powerful to him than being confident. When he was dialed in during warm-up and was ultra confident, he would kind of assume he would be dominant during the game. This created a carelessness that hurt his performance. When he was not his best in warm up, he realized he would need to be extra present that day. This often helped him perform even better than the days he was really confident.

With *Inner Excellence,* we focus on being fully present—fully engaged, heart, mind, and body—more than confidence. The ultimate confidence is not to trust yourself, someone who's prone to mistakes. It's to be fully present to the truth of what's possible and that God's got you no matter what.

Self-confidence and self-reliance go hand in hand with indifference. Self-confidence becomes self-reliance... self-reliance becomes pride... and pride becomes indifference—the opposite of love. When we're confident in ourselves it easily leads to trying to control what we cannot, separating us from God, from others, and from our true selves in the process. Fear becomes a constant threat.

Oh man, if I'm honest, that's been me most of my life. I've been caught up in my own needs and desires and treated those as more important than the suffering and needs of others.

Recently I was golfing in Vancouver, BC, with someone I had just met. As the day went on, I noticed a few times that he wasn't following the normal etiquette for golf. I was starting to get a little annoyed, when suddenly I remembered: when we'd met, I'd learned that his wife was dying of cancer. I'd forgotten all about that and was concerned about the most trivial thing that affected me—not at all about his dying wife. Ouch.

This experience—as much as I hate to say it—is a glimpse of where my heart has been. Over the years pride and fear created an indifference in me that's narrowed my vision and reduced my compassion. I've been the one Martin Luther King Jr. wrote about from jail, the white moderate who's been more devoted to order than to justice:

> *I have almost reached the regrettable conclusions that the Negro's great stumbling block in the stride toward freedom is not the White Citizen's Council-er or the Ku Klux Klanner, but the white moderate who is more devoted to "order" than to justice; who prefers a negative peace which is the absence of tension to a positive peace which is the presence of justice...*

The default in human nature is to focus on self, and we always lean towards comfort vs discomfort, status quo rather than change. Self-preservation and security easily takes the highest place in the human hierarchy of values. When self or success, career or comfort is your god, you'll do everything you can to avoid risking that treasure, especially when there's no payoff for self.

What about you? Where have you been indifferent?

God Intervened

As God watched us become more and more self-centered, unconcerned in word and deed to those in despair, he knew we were headed towards self-destruction. His heart broke and something had to be done.

God created us to join him in perfect harmony, unconditional love, and endless joy. He knew, however, that we couldn't be close to God with a heart of indifference. So, after countless years of self-centered lovers of self, God knew he had to intervene, otherwise we could never enter into his kingdom.

But what could he do?

God is a god of justice, so evil must be dealt with. So, God did something extraordinary. He sent his son down to earth, to show us in person, how much he loved us. When you truly love someone and have something important to say, it needs to be in person. Jesus came in human form to show us how to love, even your enemies, even unto death. He sacrificed his life so we could live. One perfect man died to atone for all of mankind's sin. All this so we could join him in eternal paradise.

The Ultimate Choice

Justice was set in motion when the Son of God, the King of the Universe, came to earth as a baby. However, his entrance was completely opposite of earthly kings. Of course being Creator of the Universe, he could have been born in a palace. But the only person in history who got to choose his birth, life, and death, chose to be born in a barn, live as a homeless, unpaid teacher, and then suffer a horrible, tortuous death. All by choice. All because of his infinite love for us.

Now let's take a look at how it was actually religious leaders who delivered the fatal blow to this "heathen" Jew who wouldn't bow down to their righteous rules.

> "There is one vice of which no man in the world is free; which every one in the world loathes when he sees it in someone else; and of which hardly any people, except Christians, ever imagine that they are guilty themselves. [...] There is no fault which makes a man more unpopular, and no fault which we are more unconscious of in ourselves.[...]The vice I am talking of is Pride or Self-Conceit: and the virtue opposite to it, in Christian morals, is called Humility... According to Christian teachers, the essential vice, the utmost evil, is Pride. Unchastity, anger, greed, drunkenness, and all that, are mere flea bites in comparison: it was through Pride that the devil became the devil: Pride leads to every other vice: it is the complete anti-God state of mind."
>
> — CS Lewis, *Mere Christianity*

The End of Religion (as we know it)

Religion was quite a big deal 2,000 years ago. It was the fabric woven into the culture, part of everyday life. To be a respectable citizen, one had to go to the temple, offer animal sacrifices, and have a priest who would talk to god or the gods for you. If you didn't adhere to their precise religious rituals, you might be killed.

The religious leaders were the power brokers of the day. They controlled the finances and the people and were at the top of the hierarchy, just below the king. These priests were very protective of the religious law, the one that demanded strict observance and allegiance.

The temple was where God was, and so to enter the temple, there were rigorous protocols: animal sacrifice and priests were needed to oversee and intervene for you.

Then Jesus came along and cleared out the temple. He got rid of religion and all of its status and hierarchy, guilt and shame. He brought an entirely new way of living to the world, completely opposite of the culture of the day. Rather than religious rituals offered to God or the gods, Jesus declared sacrificial, unconditional love for others (even your enemies) as the way to worship God. It was so different from what the priests taught.

And not only that... *When Jesus came to earth, he hung out with the outcasts... prostitutes, thieves, and lepers.*

This non-conformist behavior, hanging out with sinners, was complete heresy. Such a low-class thing to do. Because of this however, the lowly ones embraced Jesus and his unconditional, not-an-ounce-of-judgment love. And, most importantly, it was the lowly ones who ultimately received the life-transformation that God himself was sharing, because their hearts were humble enough to receive his love.

Jesus said:
Drop all that religious stuff.
I am the temple.
I am the priest.
I am the sacrifice.
Now all you need is me.

The message of Jesus was completely revolutionary and unimaginable.

It was a message of freedom based on a personal, intimate relationship with God Almighty. It was the anti-religion.

Jesus didn't come to create a new religion but to end religion once and for all. (Or at least re-define it: true religion switched from guilt and shame from breaking man-made laws to looking after orphans and widows and keeping oneself from being consumed by the world.)

The sacrilegious message of Jesus was so contradictory and antithetical to the religion of the day, early Christians were called atheists.

They prayed to a God you couldn't see and didn't sacrifice animals or require priests—anyone could connect with God at any time—and they did without the required idols, rituals, or golden calves.

The Religious Leaders Revolt

The religious leaders were irate. They had political power and wielded guilt and shame and punishment to great effect. Then Jesus came and shook everything up. He came as a humble king, to end hierarchy, status, and judgment. The religious leaders didn't like this radical revolution.

So, like most leaders threatened with being stripped of their power, the high priests were furious. They schemed night and day to kill Jesus. Of course, God (and Jesus) knew this would happen. It's human nature, and it would fulfill God's promises.

One day the religious leaders accomplished their goal. They killed the Son of God. However, what they thought was the end, was actually the beginning. What looked like a terrible loss for humanity, as so often happens in our own lives, was the greatest victory ever won.

Easter

On a Friday afternoon, 2,000 years ago, Jesus was killed on a cross, a perfect man willing to suffer and take the punishment we deserve. Taking on a pain that we'll never fully understand, he accepted complete (though temporary) separation from God. A few days later he rose from the dead. He conquered death and evil and wiped away our sins. Now he's in heaven, where he's prepared eternal paradise for you and I and everyone who chooses to accept his love.

All of Christianity hinges on his death and resurrection. If you can prove it didn't happen, you would disprove all of Christianity. But as history shows, it did. And that, is very, very good news.

Had you been there on the mountain that day, you may have looked up at Jesus's body hanging on the cross and thought this was the worst thing that could ever happen. And yet you were staring at the greatest thing that ever happened in world history.

Victory over death. Eternal paradise prepared for all who believe, regardless of who you are or what you've done.

What his sacrifice means

Once Jesus was killed, willingly giving up his life when he could have easily stopped it, the price was paid. Justice was served. All of humanity's evils, past and future—and evil itself—was conquered. Now we can freely enter into God's kingdom, here on earth, and forever in heaven.

When you accept God's love and give your heart to him, this means two very important things: You've now been adopted, and as author John Mark Comer says, you're now an apprentice.

Adoption

When you're born into this world, you have a natural father and mother who may or may not have planned you or even wanted you. But when you choose to accept God's love and give your life to him, you become adopted by God. As an adopted child, you receive everything a natural born baby would receive, and when you're chosen by him, you get everything that comes along with it:

- A Father that loves you more than you can imagine, and there's nothing you've ever done or could do that would change it. Even if you have no plans to walk with him, he still loves you with an infinite, outrageous, unconditional love.
- Direct connection to God and all of creation (no priest required).

Apprenticeship

"Jesus is not looking for converts to Christianity, he's looking for apprentices in the kingdom of God. Apprentices of Jesus are those who sign up for his training program... who intentionally arrange their lives around the goal of spiritual growth and maturity. Non-apprentices of Jesus are those who intentionally arrange their lives around anything else." – John Mark Comer

An apprentice is a student learning by practical experience under an expert. When Jesus came, he invited us to a life of apprenticeship with him. It's an entirely new way to live, one where your greatest goal is to become like your teacher—God himself—the one who came to earth to show you in person how to love. This means intentionally arranging your life around learning and growing every day in love, wisdom, and courage; letting go of your limitations so you can grab onto his unlimited power.

PART II

Amazing Awaits

How to Get the Best Possible Life

"We cannot find Him unless we know we need Him. We forget this need when we take a self-sufficient pleasure in our own good works. The poor and helpless are the first to find Him."
— Thomas Merton, *No Man is an Island*

To receive God's grace and get started with the best possible life, you must simply become like a little kid. When given free gifts, kids don't ask why or suggest they don't deserve it. They happily accept the lollipop without a moment's hesitation.

The God of the universe fiercely wants your heart, to lavish his sacrificial, outrageous, unconditional love on you. But like a marriage, it must be a choice. You must make the decision to accept his love. And the only way you can do that is to let go of what you've been clinging to, your lesser gods, and open your arms to receive his great love.

This is the toughest part: to let go of self-reliance, self-protection, and self-promotion. Those one-time helpful things that helped you navigate life's challenges have become the greatest obstacle to the freedom you were created for.

Seek success or money or achievements as your highest goal and you'll never be satisfied, continually striving yet never arriving. You'll constantly be anxious about what you have and might lose, or don't have and may never get. But seek first absolute fullness of life, and no matter how talented or untalented you are, every good thing will be added to you.

It's the fundamental law of the universe:

Cling to your life and lose it; give up your life and gain it.

When you hold tightly to your life, you die a thousand deaths, running when no one's chasing, hiding when you don't need to hide, protecting when nothing's threatening. But it doesn't have to be this way.

You were meant for so much more than the world can offer. To gain this life you need much more than you can produce with your limited strength. As humans we have too many fears and wounds to experience fullness of life on our own in a wounded world.

Perhaps you're wondering if it's true, that God created the universe with you in mind, and lived and died for you. Maybe you're considering if it's time to get your heart right, to see if he'll take the lead in your life. If you're sincere, then he will, because it's who he is. It's his nature. He loves you because he loves you, period. There's nothing you've ever done or could ever do that would change his love for you.[2] He is love itself and that will never, ever change.

Or perhaps you're wondering if God could really love someone like you, if he could really forgive someone who's done what you've done. Consider two great leaders from the Bible, King David, the shepherd who killed Goliath, and Moses, the leader who God used to part the Red Sea. Both were murderers. In fact, David slept with a married woman (whose husband was extremely loyal to the King) and then had him killed. Actually David had multiple people killed to ensure the loyal husband died so he could steal his wife.

While David and Moses each paid a heavy price for their terrible deeds, both were completely forgiven. Remember this: God knows you're human. He knows how weak you are. It doesn't matter what you've done. What matters is what he's done—he died for you and paid the hefty price that you should have paid.

A choice awaits. Will you accept God's love and along with it a personal relationship with the creator of the universe? Will you ask him to forgive your self-centeredness and come into your heart to run your life? It starts by having a heart-to-heart conversation with God (as you understand him). It's trusting that a power far greater than your own awaits you—the same power that makes the sun rise, sets the moon in place, and fills the forests with flowers, is ready to create a life for you beyond your imagination.

You might say something like this:

---

[2] C.S. Lewis says that either you'll submit to God's way, or he'll let you have your way—it's all up to you. "There are only two kinds of people in the end: those who say to God, 'Thy will be done,' and those to whom God says, in the end, 'Thy will be done.' All that are in Hell, choose it. Without that self-choice there could be no Hell. No soul that seriously and constantly desires joy will ever miss it. Those who seek find. To those who knock it is opened." (C.S. Lewis, The Great Divorce)

Dear God,

I don't know how to approach you or talk to you, but I want to receive your love. Please forgive me for the self-centered life I've lived. Come into my heart and take over my life. Show me who you are. Help me understand the depth of your love for me. I want to know you and be filled with your love, wisdom, and courage.

In Jesus name,
Amen

For those who have many possessions or important roles or a certain status, this sort of prayer may feel out of reach. The prayer is saying you're ready to give up your attachments and control and image and well, everything. It means handing your life over to someone whom you've just met and who could take it all away from you. It's not just scary, it's too big a leap for many. Of course it's the best decision you could ever make. It's handing over the chalk so Einstein can teach the class instead of your two-year-old self.

What this means

When you ask God into your heart to run your life, it's acknowledging to God that he can do it better than you. It's not asking the Creator of the Universe to be your assistant. It's an apprenticeship... a completely new way of life, starting fresh, with God leading every decision. In this life, your faith and trust is in God, not *your* skills or circumstances or results.

When you dedicate your life to apprenticeship, to training for heart transformation, everything changes. Now every day, every situation, is here to teach you and help you, learn to serve God, love your enemies, and care for the poor.

You may still keep the same job, it will just be with a new ultimate goal. Rather than striving for personal success, your work becomes one of the primary ways you learn and grow in your apprenticeship. It becomes a means of expressing God's love—so you *become* the expression of God's love. Rather than simply a way to pay the bills or be successful, your daily labor becomes a path for you to practice how to love and how to serve—how to be selfless and therefore fearless.

As you learn and grow, self-confidence won't have the same attraction it once did. In fact, your goal will be to not rely on self at all. You're trusting God, knowing that no matter how your circumstances and results turn out, he's got you. It's not that now when you pray God will give you what you want. It's that now when you pray, you pray more for wisdom than anything else, because you realize that you don't know what's best for you, but you know that he knows, and more than anything, you want to know him. Because in growing to know him, you become more like him.

To grow in faith and belief is to recognize that you don't know what's best for you but God does, and he always works to help you become the person you were born to become.

Imagine you're the uncle of five-year-old Boaz. Do you give little Boaz whatever he wants? That would not be loving, would it? What if he begs and begs to play on the highway? The answer is a strict no, not today, not ever. That's how love is. Unconditional love has strict boundaries. It gives the person what's best for them, not necessarily what they want. That's what God does for you, and sometimes, you may be really upset about it.

Occasionally you get the opposite of what you pray for, and it really hurts. It doesn't mean things are not going how they should, in fact everything may be unfolding perfectly. When it looks like the very worst has happened, it may be precisely that the very best thing has happened.

Just like on a Friday afternoon 2,000 years ago when the very best person in the land was betrayed and murdered, it appeared to be the worst possible scenario. Appearances can be deceiving, however. This horrible thing set the stage for the greatest act of love in human history and the greatest thing that ever happened to the human race.

When you give your heart to God you no longer judge things by outward appearances, but instead you walk by faith, not by sight. You're stepping into the extraordinary, unfolding story that God slowly reveals to you. It's the most freeing, incredible way to live. A changing of the guard. A change of heart.

Heart Transformation: Total Renovation

"Imagine yourself as a living house. God comes in to rebuild that house. At first, perhaps, you can understand what he is doing. He is getting the drains right and stopping the leaks in the roof and so on; you knew that those jobs needed doing and so you are not surprised. But presently He starts knocking the house about in a way that hurts abominably and does not seem to make any sense. What on earth is he up to? The explanation is that he is building quite a different house from the one you thought of - throwing out a new wing here, putting on an extra floor there, running up towers, making courtyards. You thought you were being made into a decent little cottage: but he is building a palace. He intends to come and live in it Himself."

— C.S. Lewis, *Mere Christianity*

How to Think About the Best Possible Life

Imagine a light switch on the wall. Flip the switch and the room fills with light. Flip it again, and the room goes dark. It's like magic. A single flip of a switch can light up an entire stadium. However, no matter how much light fills the space, the switch is not the source of the power. It's only the means through which the power flows. The switch in and of itself is useless; it needs the energy to flow through it to be useful. This is the Christian life—the best possible one.

No matter how hard you try on your own, no matter how many stadiums you fill, none of it was your own doing. On your own, you're a switch on a wall. A small, lifeless piece of plastic. When you surrender your life to God, however, and continue to learn how to do that every day, anything is possible.

The God-surrendered life has a completely different understanding of reality and success from Western culture. It blows away all our misconceptions of self-reliance and lets go of attachment to all our third world goals and dreams. While it's possible your external goals will remain the same, many readers may realize their goals are too small. Even if you keep them, as you learn and grow, your attachment to them will fade away. This is because you'll gain one singular attachment—to God himself—and all his love, joy, and peace.

In your self-reliant life, as David Foster Wallace said, you worshipped something. You cannot not worship. There's been some thing, some person, some status or success or feeling that you've been worshipping, that you've devoted your life to. That's what you've been attached to, and we are formed by what we attach to. So... what's been forming *you*?

When you let go of your attachment to your lesser god, you get to be transformed by the God who created you and everything around you. You get to share in his power, beauty, and grace and you get to be yourself—your true self. As you grow, you'll become less attached to your results and circumstances and more attached to God and his love for all humanity. Your vision will expand and so will what's possible in your life.

God is inviting you to a life of freedom and fulfillment, independent of how skilled or successful you are or what your situation is. The only prerequisite is to let God transform your heart and take control of your life, surrendering everything to him. The God of the universe (who created you with an extraordinary purpose in mind) will run your life now.

This life, as C.S. Lewis said, is not the life you're used to and likely not the one you expect. Your heart is not the house being renovated into a decent little cottage. Your walls are getting torn down because a palace is being built—for the King himself to live in. This total renovation is far beyond any notion of what you might imagine right now. In whatever time you have left on earth, if you make the best decision you could ever make (give God complete control of your life), you might anticipate a few things:

- A life of adventure. One where you're continually course-correcting, getting caught up in the desires and fears of this tangible world. Then, bringing yourself back to the Truth of who God is and therefore who you are, what he's done for you, what he's prepared for you, and where he is right now (holding your right hand).

- A life of humility, which is *an accurate view of self*. Humility is to not think too high of yourself (inflated) or too low of yourself (deflated) since both ultimately lead to self-rejection (because they're inaccurate). Humility is to understand the truth about who you are and why you were created. It's the recognition that God gave you everything and you have nothing to offer back except your heart and your effort. When you're truly humble, you can never be humiliated. It's the selfless and therefore fearless way you were created to live.

- A life in community. When you recognize and respond to God's love, you're joining in with the saints of the past and present, on the same path, studying, praying, and serving with them as you grow together. It's a mutual devotion to serving God and others, placing others as more important than yourself. In this life, sacrificial love sparks the joy you were created for.

- A life where your heart, formerly pulled in every direction, divided by competing loves and desires, now has one unifying desire: to become undivided—wholehearted. This means to love most what's most empowering, which is love itself (God). Your greatest desires change from enriching yourself and your family, to empowering and enriching the poorest of the poor as well as serving and loving the most wretched, and even your enemies—because you're no better than them.

- A life of daily surrender, where your heart transforms from self-centered needs, impulses, and desires to the flow of resonance. This is where your urges, compulsions, and longings get more aligned with your purpose (love God and love others, for example). When you flow with resonance, you live in non-judgmental awareness and gratitude, not continually judging circumstances and reacting emotionally. This is because your life is God's to do with as he sees fit. Your life is not your responsibility.

- A life with one foot in joy and one foot in suffering. It's offering everything you have: your time and energy as well as all your resources and your very life—to God, others, and even those who oppose you.

- A life spent in the realization that the greatest need in the world is for *me* to let go of *my own* preoccupation with self and that the worst evil is the pride in my own heart and the self-reliance and indifference that go along with it.

- The life of a disciplined student, an apprentice, where your highest daily goal is to learn and grow to get to know Jesus, so you can be like him and love like him. As your connection with God grows, so does every other area in your life.

- A new way of living—including a devotion to serving the immigrant and refugee, the imprisoned and hungry, the orphan and widow. Now your citizenship is in heaven. There's no more borders—racial, national, or otherwise. Every life has equal value, no matter what country, race, or ethnic background. You are the hands and feet of God himself, having the honor of sharing his sacrificial, outrageous, unconditional love.

When you surrender your life to God, you're handing the reigns over to the Creator of the universe. It's not just magical—it's electric.

The Fairy Tale of the Witch and the Travelers

Tim Keller tells a story in his book *The Prodigal Prophet*...

Years ago, I read an old fairy tale about a wicked witch who lived in a remote cottage in the deep forest. When travelers came through looking for lodging, she offered them a meal and a bed. It was the most wonderfully comfortable bed any of them had ever felt. But it was a bed full of deep magic, and if you were asleep in it when the sun came up you would turn to stone. Then you became a figure in the witch's statuary, trapped until the end of time. The witch forced a young girl to serve her, and though she had no power to resist the witch, the girl had become more and more filled with pity for her victims.

One day a young man came looking for bed and board and was taken in. The servant girl could not bear to see him turned to stone. So she threw sticks, stones, and thistles into his bed. It made the bed horribly uncomfortable. Every time he turned he felt a new painful object under him. Though he cast each one out, there was always a new one to dig into his flesh. He slept only fitfully and rose feeling weary and worn, long before dawn. As he walked out the front door, the servant girl met him, and he berated her cruelly. "How could you give a traveler such a terrible bed full of sticks and stones?" he cried and went on his way.

"Ah," she said under her breath, "The misery you know now is nothing like the infinitely greater misery a comfortable sleep would have brought upon you! Those were my sticks and stones of love."

Keller continues: "God puts sticks and stones of love in our beds to wake us up, to bring us to rely on him, lest the end of history or of life overtake us without the Lord in our heart, and we be turned to stone."

How to Live the Best Possible Life

Give us, O Lord, a steadfast heart, which no unworthy affection may drag downwards; give us an unconquered heart, which no tribulation can wear out; give us an upright heart, which no unworthy purpose may tempt aside. Bestow upon us also, O Lord our God, understanding to know you, diligence to seek you, wisdom to find you, and a faithfulness that may finally embrace you; through Jesus Christ our Lord.

— Thomas Aquinas

The best possible life is not a life of leisure, sitting around a campfire listening to Taylor Swift and Justin Bieber (if that's your thing). There's work to be done, which is a wonderful thing, because it's why you were created. We come alive when we immerse ourselves in the work we're fashioned to do. So… what's the work?

The work to do is this:

believe.

Believe that God is who he says he is. Believe his promises. Believe what the Bible says about who you are and what he's prepared for you. To live the best possible life is to have a heart that believes the Truth about your life and all that's possible for you.

To believe all that can be difficult, because it requires surrendering your current beliefs. Right now, you have certain beliefs about yourself and the world and your place in it. For most of us, those beliefs, perhaps unknowingly, have been built up by fear, bounded by barriers of self-protection.

Most people work long hours every day, every week, to get things for themselves and their families. They work to have money in the bank so they can feel secure, evidenced by a decent place to live, good food to eat, and a less stressful life. If they work hard and things work out, then perhaps they'll explore new experiences and travel to distant lands. We work so we can build a life.

What I'm asking you to consider, what God is asking you, is would you consider building a life that goes beyond *your own* desires and fears, beyond anything you've ever imagined?

Before you answer, consider the cost. The life that God offers you is an extraordinary one, but it means a complete restructuring of your heart, all your loves, and well, your entire life. It means loving your enemies. It means serving the poor, caring for the marginalized, and living completely opposite of how the world says you should. It can be pretty scary.

It takes the willingness to step into the dark alley where all your fears lie, where you're completely alone, putting your trust in God rather than your abilities or connections or finances. That takes belief.

Let's say you want to believe that you can live with deep contentment, joy, and confidence no matter what, but you've never lived that way. Or that if you surrender your life to God, that he'll take care of you and carry you to the end.

The reason most of us haven't lived the life we were designed for is that our beliefs have not lined up with our true selves, the person we're created to be. We've been caught up in our own stories, living in self-protection and self-reliance, limiting the love we're able to receive and give.

Love is the greatest power in the universe—it's what empowers belief in God. The more you soak up God's love, the more belief you gain—about who God is and therefore who you are, what he's doing in the world and how you can join in.

It takes courage to believe in something other than yourself because that means letting go of control. If you want real courage, you can gain it, but... you need to be honest about your past, willing to face your fears, let go of your pride and who you've been, and live for a purpose greater than yourself, greater even than your own well-being.

Courage is the foundation of belief. It takes courage to act on the Truth rather than your fears or feelings. It's giving up your past and the stories you've created about your life and being present to the Truth of who God is and who you are. It's not a trait you're born with. It's something you choose. We can't all win Olympic gold medals or play in the NFL, but we can all believe in what we cannot see, that we can become someone we've never been. We can all choose to trust, to have faith, to be courageous.

The Instruction Manual

One of the primary resources you're given is a life instruction book called the Bible. It's a story of redemption, filled with God's words, desires, and directions on how to live. You'll learn the guidelines to navigate a complex and unstable world. The Bible contains the wisdom of the universe. The more the words get embedded into your mind and deep in your heart, the more reality you'll see and beauty you'll experience.

Just like God created the universe with scientific laws like gravity and thermodynamics, he also created principles that empower you to function at your highest level, a level closely connected to God. The instructions, as you'll see, revolve around relationships: to God, yourself, others, and your work.

God knows that we have a human (self-centered) nature and that we need help, structure, and boundaries to live an extraordinary life. We need a transformed heart, one like his. So, we have our time on earth to enable this transformation, to embrace his perfectly wholehearted presence within us while our human nature gets transformed.

Two Great Loves

Jesus was asked by an expert in the law, "Of all the commandments, which are the most important?" He answered:

1. Love God with all your heart, all your mind, all your strength and all your soul.
2. Love your neighbor as yourself.

The Work: Do. Love. Walk.

The Bible shares three primary directives (requirements for the best possible life):

1. Do justice.
2. Love kindness.
3. Walk humbly.

Do Justice

Jesus was asked by an expert in the law how to inherit eternal life. He answered with the same two commands (love God with your whole heart and love your neighbor as yourself). The expert then asked, "Who is my neighbor?" Instead of answering directly, he told a story.

A man was traveling down a dangerous road where lots of criminals hung out and he was attacked and left for dead. A few religious people walked by and avoided him. A person of an opposing ethnic group however, stopped to help, putting himself in danger. He cared for him as if he were family, took him to a hotel, and paid for him to stay several weeks. Then he told the hotel owner to take care of him however he saw fit and that he'd reimburse him when he come back in a month. This is how Jesus said to love your neighbor.

In other words, stop everything you're doing and love others (even your enemy) so much that you put yourself in danger and risk your life. Then open your bank account to the stranger. It doesn't make sense.

How can that be wise, to take so much time and energy away from your worthy goals to sacrifice so much (perhaps your very life) for an enemy? Seems so irresponsible and illogical. The truth is, it's not logical, not in the normal third world way of life. That's because a Christian doesn't follow the "normal" ways of living. For a Christian, this life on earth is very temporary. It's the training ground for your heart. It's a way of doing life that is truly an illogical, sacrificial, outrageously spendthrift way to live—the way of Christ.

As a God of justice, God is extremely concerned with the heartbroken and disadvantaged. There's five special groups that he singles out that we should be particularly loving towards:

1. Widows
2. Orphans
3. Immigrants
4. Prisoners
5. Poor and marginalized

Jesus said when you take care of the least of these people, you take care of me. When you're indifferent to them, you're indifferent to me. Because God loves all people with his sacrificial, outrageous, unconditional love, there must be justice.

Love Kindness

The way of Christ is to love so fully and deeply that you willingly sacrifice your own life for others, even those actively opposing you. It means to be radically generous in all you do—even to give to all who ask—in a way that loves them the best you know how. It means to forgive those who've wronged you such that you view your shortcomings as greater than theirs—no matter what they've done.

To love kindness is to love like Christ loved. When you realize that you're far more lost and wicked than you can comprehend and yet immensely more loved than you can possibly imagine, you can love like Christ loved. You can love the stranger and the immigrant, the poor, needy and imprisoned, and even your enemies, with the love that he gives you.

Perhaps the most powerful way to love others and be kind is to share your life with them. It's one thing to give a stranger on the street ten dollars; it's an entirely different and far more impactful thing to invite them into your home for a meal.

Walk Humbly

As a child of God, chosen before the creation of the world, you were created to do great things. The incredible reality of humility is that the more humble you are (i.e. the more accurate your view of self is), the more God can work in your life and the more courage and belief you'll have.

Consider Moses from the Bible—the most humble man in the world. He was also a murderer with a speech impediment. Yet, with an accurate view of self (and God's mercy), he stood up to Pharaoh, led his people out of Egypt (after 400 years of slavery) and parted the Red Sea.

When you're truly humble, you become unstoppable because defeat doesn't derail you and success doesn't inflate you. When we feel we're the ones responsible for our own lives, we take failure personally and easily get deflated. The same thing happens with success: we think it was our doing and so we become more self-reliant. As you may recall, self-reliance leads to pride, pride leads to indifference and indifference distances you from God and everything good. When we rely more on self, we simultaneously rely less on God.

The problem is that there can only be one thing in your life in which you place your ultimate trust. It's either God or something else. The only thing it can't be is both.

The Michael Phelps Principle

Over the course of his career, the American swimmer Michael Phelps won more Olympic gold medals (23) than most countries have won in their entire history. Pretty incredible, right? My question to you is, how much of that was his doing? How much was he responsible for, and how much was God responsible for? Think about your answer in terms of a percentage. For example, 50/50 would mean it was 50% Phelps and 50% God.

In other words, when we evaluate one of the most prolific success stories in sports history, what's the truth about how it happened?

Phelps went five straight years without missing a single day of workouts. He swam the laps, had the early mornings, suffered, and sacrificed. He dedicated his life to training. So, does he deserve 75% of the credit? Obviously, he could have sat on the couch all day. Perhaps it's 90%?

This is an important question, because where you place the credit has a huge impact on the amount of gratitude you have. And we're only grateful when we feel we're given gifts. If we feel we're the ones that are successful or responsible for our outcomes, then we're less grateful (and also prone to anxiety since we're also the ones causing the mistakes and failures).

When we're consistently grateful however, we're not only resonating with a powerful, positive energy, we're also developing inner peace. Inner peace is a huge component of inner strength, which is the primary component of mental toughness.

Think of it this way. What are the most important factors that contributed to Phelps' success? Let's start with his body, his training, and his mind/mental toughness. Where did he get the DNA and body type suited for long, powerful strokes? From his parents. Well, what role did he have in choosing his parents?

Now imagine he had the same parents, but he was born 400 years ago in Afghanistan. What are the chances he wins twenty-three gold medals? It's 0.00%. There were no Olympic Games 400 years ago. Likely he would have been a peasant, spending his days searching for food.

How important was the body he was born with and the country and century he was born in? Well, without getting all three right, he's got no chance.

Michael Phelps, because of his hard work, willingness to face his fears and suffer for extended periods of time, definitely had a role to play. In his free will, he chose to do the work. He chose to suffer. But where did he get the mind that could believe he could one day be great, and thus push himself to get there?

Phelps definitely deserves credit for all that he sacrificed, and so do you. But how much? The answer I would give, percentage-wise, is two. Two percent (with God being responsible for the other 98%). We could call this the 98:2 principle.

So...if it's true that one of the greatest achievements in sports history can overwhelmingly be attributed to gifts from God—what about success in your life?

When we start taking credit (at least internally) for the successes or good things in our lives, we start to have an inaccurate view of self. This inaccurate lens becomes a veil of ignorance through which we lose the ability to see the truth about who God is and, therefore, who we are. It leads us to believe in ourselves and our little strength rather than God and his unlimited power.

With these faulty beliefs, we're a little more unsteady, and so we feel the need to control what we cannot, which leads us to take more and more things personally. We get offended when we feel disrespected, embarrassed when we feel foolish, and irritated when we don't get what we want. We become narrow-minded, distracted, and indifferent.

The Selfless and therefore Fearless Life

The biggest obstacle in performance and in life is getting in our own way. Our self-centered lives create fear and anxiety as we try to control what we cannot. This is because we feel pressure to get the results and circumstances we feel we need to be ok.

When you give your life to God however, you're no longer the one in charge. You belong to him. You're no longer responsible for meeting your needs (or your family's needs). You're not the provider. You can relax.

Your responsibility is for your heart and your effort. The rest is up to God. The more you let God into your heart (your control center), the more he can do in your life and the more joy you can have.

When we're running our lives, we tend to over-analyze all the circumstances because there's so much out of our control. In today's world of instability and violence, it's very hard to give up control. You can either stare at your circumstances and let anxiety consume you, or you can focus on God and let his love flow through you.

The more selfless you are, or "self-forgetful" as Tim Keller says, the more fearless you are. The more willing you are to face your fears, to embrace them, and trust Jesus with them, the more free you become.

When you're selfless, your fears begin to move from self-protection to self-surrender. The One who holds the oceans in place becomes the one you fear—the good kind of fear—the kind that keeps you focused and filled with awe and wonder. This allows you to maintain an accurate view of self, where you can be sufficiently grateful, and when you're grateful, then you have inner peace. Inner peace is powerful because it's the foundation for inner strength and mental toughness.

When you have inner peace, you go out into the world in strength, no matter how crazy or unstable your circumstances are. But when your inner world is in shambles, you go out into the world in weakness, no matter how many millions of followers or dollars you have.

The selfless and therefore fearless life is a life of inner peace, which lays the foundation for courage. Courage is the fuel for belief. It allows us to slow down and create space in our lives to soak up God's love.

When you believe (that is, when you have a subconscious comfort level) that God has got you no matter what, then your excitement grows to be used by God... to do justice, love kindness, and walk humbly. And the more you do those things, the more aligned you are with the waves and the wind, the sun and the sea, and everything in between.

The Only Way to Victory

" Exalted high in victory. Bent low in surrender. The two postures seem opposite, but Jesus understood that if you want to experience victory, you must start in surrender. Surrender brings power, and the need to surrender is deeply tied to Jesus' offer of living in the flow of the Spirit. You receive power through the act of surrender that you cannot obtain any other way; you receive freedom through submission that you will otherwise never know... Amazingly enough, the most powerful tool against the most powerful addiction in the world never asks people to decide to stop doing what is destroying their lives. Instead of mobilizing the will, its followers surrender their will. Try to overcome the problem by your will, and it will beat you. Surrender your will, and sobriety becomes possible. Surrender, which we think means defeat, turns out to be the only way to victory. This is not just the case with alcohol. It is also true with other addictions, with habits, with brokenness — and with sin in general."

— John Ortberg, *The Me I Want to Be*

How to Train Your Heart

You can't change merely by changing your thinking, or through great acts of the will, but rather by changing what you love most. Change happens not only by giving your mind new truths — though it does involve that — but also by feeding the imagination new beauties so you love Jesus supremely. We change when we change what we worship the most.

— Tim Keller

In my life, I've loved some pretty amazing things: baseball and football, camping and fishing, long summer days, strategy board games, sushi, Thai curry, Korean BBQ... You know, all the best things in life. And golf, of course.

As great as those things are, they're lower-level-loves. They're wonderful, amazing gifts to experience, but they're all third world loves—awesome but temporary. Sweet, but solely circumstantial.

Most of my life I've chased lesser loves. I'm not saying that I loved liver and onions or pro wrestling (as great as those things may be). I'm saying that what I loved most, with all my heart, was something unstable and transitory. I dreamed of hitting home runs and being the one everyone admired. But so much of that was out of my control. And since what I loved most was unstable, I was unstable. And when I lost it, I lost everything.

We're made to love and be loved, and yet we so easily fall for lesser loves. We give in to inferior desires.

Here's how it works:

Since we're created by God and for God, we have a deep desire for his unconditional love and the joy that comes from it. We're born with a craving for *his* type of love and connection, the deepest, most extraordinary kind. But, since as humans, we're led around by our eyes, what we see captures our attention. Although we only see the tip of the iceberg, less than 10% of reality, this is what we experience as real—as if it's *all* of reality—a world of temporary transactions and superficial satisfactions.

We act as if the third world is all there is. Our lives have come down to what we experience with our senses. Of course, if this is all there is, the obvious choice would be to maximize what we can see and feel and taste. But then we eventually realize that chasing pleasure and increasingly better life circumstances—the Hollywood dream—a life of comfort, ease, and admiration, is not the true dream (unless you want to become an addict, needing more and more sensations to have less and less joy).

Combine this senses-led orientation together with a self-centered ego that's always threatened, continuously comparing, and never satisfied... and you have a recipe for a deep longing that constantly gets caught up in what looks amazing but always turns out empty.

This is the great challenge. To be human is to have a self-centered nature, an ego that's always threatened, a body that always wants comfort, a mind that creates untrue stories, and a heart that craves a love and connection unavailable in the world as we know it.

On your own, you're naturally self-centered heart will forever be divided, endlessly chasing better circumstances and results, trying to build a better life, seeking the love you crave. You'll always be searching but never finding. Until, of course, you stop the self-reliant chase and surrender your life to the God of the universe, who's waiting for you this very moment.

The best possible life has an undivided heart, one that loves most what's most empowering. An undivided heart has one all-encompassing devotion—God himself—the source of every good thing. Its loves have been re-ordered, going from loving temporary third-world satisfactions the most, to having the creator of the universe—and everything that comes with walking with him—top the list.

The undivided heart (one that's wholehearted) has nine characteristics that are continually growing: love, joy, peace, patience, kindness, goodness, faithfulness, gentleness, and self-control.

It's a heart that's willing to sacrifice short-term pleasure for long-term gain because it has a truer and more expansive view of reality. The more reality we see (capital-T Truth), the more our desires line up with what's most empowering.

So how do we get this undivided heart with an expansive vision? How can we change from living a self-centered life, always wondering "What's in it for me", to having more awareness of the extraordinary truth of who God is and who we are—the reality of heaven?

Here's four ways:

1. Clarify your purpose.
2. Master your ego.
3. Fuel your soul.
4. Renew your mind.

Clarify Your Purpose

Whether you're an athlete, an entrepreneur, or single mother of four, you need one unifying, all-encompassing focus for your life—and it needs to be built around a broader vision than your own needs and wants. Unless you have a purpose for your life beyond yourself, you'll continually be chasing the wind, endlessly searching for better circumstances and results, caught up in self-protection, unaware of your indifference. Even if your dreams come true, like those of seven-time Super Bowl champion Tom Brady, you'll think, "God, there's got to be more than this."

So how might you go about finding your life purpose? You can start by considering a simple statement that's powerful for us all:

My purpose is to love God and love others.

You might think of it this way: you were created by God and for God and his two greatest commandments are to love him (with all your heart) and love others. (Commandments are God's ways of telling us what is absolutely necessary to live the Best

Possible Life.) Remember that unconditional love is your greatest power, your deepest need, and greatest desire. Everything you thought you ever wanted falls under unconditional love. It's in our DNA. We're designed for relationship, to love and serve in order to be filled with fullness of life.

You might start by journaling on some key areas and asking a few questions:

- How do you want to feel?
  - Whether you're an athlete or artist, musician or manager, how do you want to feel when you work? How do you want to feel in the rest of your life when you're not working or performing?
  - For my part, I want to feel deep contentment, joy, and confidence in my daily life with God—no matter what I'm doing, who I'm with, or where I am in the world.
  - To clarify how you want to feel, you might think about your favorite memories, the times when you were at your best, and recall how those times felt. Was there peace, joy, or gratitude? How would you describe it? Think of four or five words that describe how you felt then, and want to feel again.

- How do you want to live?
  - How do you want to handle adversity and the vast majority of life that you can't control?
  - When you encounter difficult times and the dark night of the soul, how do you want to respond?
  - In John Mark Comer's *Practicing the Way*, he shares a powerful quote by Martin Luther King Jr... "If a man is called to be a street sweeper, he should sweep streets even as Michelangelo painted, or Beethoven composed

music, or Shakespeare wrote poetry. He should sweep streets so well that all the hosts of heaven and earth will pause to say, 'Here lived a great street sweeper who did his job well.'"

Note: to do your job well does *not* mean getting the results you want or being successful; it means giving it your best and doing it as unto a king, even if you fail—*especially* if you fail.

- Who do you want to become?
  - Or perhaps better said, who is the person God created you to become? Consider the people you've most admired throughout history—those you've known and those you've never met, past and present. What types of people were they? How would you describe them?

You might also write in your journal about your deepest values, such as love, wisdom, courage, peace, joy, connection, etc.

Think of it like this: A solid foundation for your purpose involves powerful resources like love, peace, and joy, your greatest values, and the person you want to become—were created to become. My purpose, for example, is to share God's love, wisdom, and courage with athletes and leaders around the world. And whoever God puts in my path.

Once you write your first version of a purpose statement, to test it, ask yourself if it's something that's not dependent on circumstances. If you lose everything and everyone, could you still live your purpose? Could you do it in prison, for example? Then put it on your phone and places where you see it every day so you can live it out and use it to inform all your decisions.

Master Your Ego

Your ego is the engine behind self-centeredness and pride, the root of fear, and the depletion of your power. It's the veil that limits your vision and stunts your growth. It blocks your view of God and others, prompting you to take everything personal.

In the pursuit of self-mastery, mastering the ego is essential. To master your ego, here's three characteristics/goals to pray to become:

1. Unoffendable
2. Unembarrassable
3. Unirritable

To be unoffendable is to be completely humble. When we take offense from something someone said or did, it's usually because we feel disrespected, so we feel the need to self-protect. The problem is, at any moment some stranger could say or do something that disrespects you or your family. And with eight billion people in the world, that's a lot of looking over your shoulder guarding what you can't control. The truth is, what someone says or does reveals who they are, not who you are. And if you allow yourself to be upset from a stranger's words or actions, you'll never have peace. If you want to live a life of deep contentment, joy, and confidence no matter what, you can't let strangers take over your inner world.

To be unembarrassable is to have immense freedom. When you're willing to make mistakes or look foolish, your world opens up to possibilities. When you have to appear a certain way (perhaps in how you dress or speak or act), you'll always be wondering if you dressed or spoke or acted the proper way. You'll constantly be threatened, because at any moment, being human, you might slip up.

We get irritated when we're attached to our circumstances and physical reality. When we feel entitled, we're easily irritated. If you want to live a life of resonance, however, we need to get comfortable in a wide variety of circumstances—especially those unexpected and unwanted—not constantly judging and reacting to situations we don't like.

Think of it this way: if by a miracle from God, your life was saved today, would you be annoyed with the traffic, or someone's comment, or any other circumstance, for that matter? No—nothing would irritate you because you would be grateful just to be alive.

The common thread between all three self-mastery components is a humble heart—one that's not inflated or deflated. The humble heart has the amazing quality of behavioral flexibility, which is the ability to have peace and resonance in any situation. If you can get to the point where you have no buttons that can be pushed, where there's nothing that people can say or do (or situations that arise) that would throw you into emotional instability, that's when you have freedom.

Mastering the ego is crucial to living with deep contentment, joy, and confidence, otherwise you'll constantly be anxious about making mistakes, wondering what people think, and reacting to unexpected, unwanted situations with anger or frustration.

Fuel Your Soul

Every day you're filling your heart with thoughts and images that are programming your heart and mind. Those words, ideas, and pictures create feelings that fuel your desires and beliefs. Those desires and beliefs are running your life. Whatever you watch, read, listen to, and the people you spend time with is fueling your soul. You'll have a good idea what you've been fueling your soul with by what happens when life squeezes you.

Sure you have peace and confidence when life is good and things are easy. But what happens when you lose your job, or fail dramatically, or your greatest fear comes true? Then you'll know what's in your heart, and how it's been programmed.

So... what have *you* been fueling your soul with? What came out when *you* were squeezed? What thoughts, words, and actions were revealed in the most frustrating moments of your life?

To fuel your soul wisely means to fill your heart with what's best for you, with what can empower and sustain you. It means to listen to, watch, read about, and spend time with people, books, and ideas that bring fullness of life.

The goal is to see the realities of heaven clear enough so that you have a deep sense of awe, wonder, and respect for life itself. Then your great dream will be to connect with the one who *gives* you life—who *is* life. Here's some ways:

- Listen to wisdom-filled podcasts, sermons, and audiobooks (see *Where to go From Here*, p. 160, for ideas)
- Memorize bible passages.
    - Get deep truths into your heart so when you're squeezed, wisdom comes out. You might start with Psalm 103 (NLT).
    - Get the audio version of the bible – try *The Listener's Bible*, NIV version, narrated by Max McLean.
- Create a music playlist filled with God's words and promises.
    - Music has the power to energize and revitalize, especially when the words are in tune with the power of the universe.

- Share life with other Christians
    - If you're starting fresh, pray for groups to love and serve – that's where the apprentices hang out.

A large part of fueling your soul is sharing life with those who have the same hope; those who devote their lives to sacrificially loving God and others. With so many denominations and conflicting messages, how can you tell who to share life with and/or what group/church/community to join?

First, it may help to realize that every church has broken humans, with wounds and fears, all trying to do the best they can with what they have in their heart. Most will be just like you, trying to figure it all out while not judging others, with various levels of success at it.

As far as leadership goes and the general vibe, here's a few characteristics of a church or group that loves God with all their heart:

- They love sacrificially.

- They do justice, love kindness, and walk humbly.

- In their pursuit of justice, they have a heart of compassion for the poor and marginalized, orphan and widow, imprisoned and immigrant.

- They realize that the biggest problem in the world is the sin in their own hearts, and thus they have a keen awareness of their absolute need for God and their utter lack of anything they have to offer, except obedience, rooted in gratitude and love.

These are the types of people who God has used the most over the years. They join in with the poor in their distress and they mourn for all the evil and suffering in the world. Their hearts are broken for their complicity in the world's misery and yet their hearts are filled with joy because of the love God gives them, which they pour out to others as their offering.

They're not the smartest or most talented—but they're usually the most humble. Thus they're always seeking to learn and grow—it's their top daily goal. They crave wisdom—to know who God is and therefore who they are, what he's doing in the world and how they can join in.

Renew Your Mind

Every day when you wake up, you're immersed in world three—a world of comparison and conflict, filled with unexpected and unwanted events. Unless you're very intentional about it, you'll become more and more conformed to this world, increasing in self-concern and self-protection. In this unstable, unfair world, there's never a time when you can finally say, ok, my circumstances are set, it's all good and will stay that way. That's why most of us are continually on edge, far from the deep contentment we were created for. As humans we're easily consumed with what's in front of us, latching on to what's behind us, creating despair inside of us.

We need to be revived. Regularly. Woken up to the Truth. Revival comes from continual refreshment of your heart and mind with the Truth of who God is and therefore who you are and what's possible in your life.

It starts with being deliberate about making space in our lives—literally and figuratively—for that Truth. We need to let go of the results and circumstances we get attached to and continually pull ourselves mentally, emotionally, and physically out of the fleeting, finite third world. We need to regularly check in and stop the over-analysis, judgment, and self-concern—and everything we're doing. We need space and we need Truth.

Here's a few mental renewal tools to keep in mind:

- Keep a journal.
    - Since your new top goal is to learn and grow every day, tracking what you're learning is crucial. We need to regularly examine our lives if we want to grow.
    - Write about the gifts you've been given and the things you're learning. If you're new to journaling, you can start by just writing the topics that are on your mind, then move on to concerns and desires, gratitudes and learnings. And of course, keep dreaming. (Note: see Inner Excellence Ultimate Dream Journal in Glossary).
- Simplify your life.
    - Clarify your purpose and make sure every decision in your life is purpose-driven. The great enemy of the spiritual life is busyness. We have anxiety because we have too many thoughts from too many concerns.
- Schedule solitude.
    - Create space in your life, where you have nothing to react to or attend to besides God's love for you. Spend time in nature, with no screens.
- Ruthlessly eliminate hurry from your life.
    - Slow down. Walk slower. Drive slower. A clear mind and unburdened heart are foundational for the Best

Possible Life and this requires faith, simplicity, and prioritization—so you can think less and trust God more.
- o Take one full day off a week to listen and learn about who God is and therefore who you are. Stopping the ceaseless striving and all the work is a fundamental principle of *The Best Possible Life*. We have to regularly remind ourselves who we're trusting (God) and who we're not (ourselves).

- Serve others, especially those who cannot return the favor.
  - o When you serve in secret, like John Ortberg said, you set yourself free of the question, "What are people thinking of me?"
  - o When you sacrifice your time and energy to help someone else, your soul vibrates with love.

One of the key disciplines to renewing your mind is to make sure the words you use (in thought and conversation) are always true (about who you are and what's possible) and empowering. Beliefs are what's running your life, and those beliefs are continually being reinforced all day long by what you think, feel, and say.

Most of us struggle way too long with various challenges because we keep reinforcing limiting beliefs by the specific words we use. Here's a discipline to remember:

Speak the truth about the past to create possibilities in the future.

To speak the truth about the past means to always speak in past tense about anything you don't want to continue, and ideally speak about it in a positive manner. Your heart (and subconscious) is always listening, creating new beliefs, or most often, reinforcing limiting ones.

For example: "I'm struggling with fear and anxiety," or "I'm an anxious person," becomes "IN THE PAST, I struggled with anxiety," or even better, "In the past I've had moments where I've had peace and clarity." (Even if that was only 5% of the time, and you were anxious for the other 95%.)

When we speak of things that happened (that we don't want) in the present tense, our subconscious looks for evidence, and then a pattern, to keep it going. The limiting belief gets reinforced. However, when we speak of it as past tense, the subconscious much more readily lets it go. Your subconscious mind is always waiting for directions to make sure your energy (and vibrations) match what you say and believe.

In summary, training your heart is an everyday thing. It starts with daily prayer and surrender, surrendering to the Master (God). Your part—your 2%—is to love God and love others with your whole heart. To have an undivided heart, one that's aware of what you've been given and what's possible, is to have an imagination consumed with what's most extraordinary and beautiful. This will enable you to let go of the past and lead you to your potential: the glorious riches of unlimited faith and possibilities.

How to Let Go of Your Attachments

Do not depend on the hope of results. You may have to face the fact that your work will be apparently worthless and even achieve no result at all, if not perhaps results opposite to what you expect. As you get used to this idea, you start more and more to concentrate not on the results, but on the value, the rightness, the truth of the work itself.
— Thomas Merton, *Letter to a Young Activist*

Imagine you're an artist, and you want to create the most extraordinary piece of art that's ever been created. How would you go about starting this project? Would you not want to spend time in the presence of the greatest works of art ever produced? Perhaps you'd fly to Paris to see Da Vinci's *Mona Lisa* at the Louvre. Then you might head to the Santa Maria delle Grazie in Milan to see *The Last Supper*. And maybe you'd swing by New York City's Museum of Modern Art to experience *Starry Night*.

When your mind gets hold of beauties it's never seen before or knew existed, it never goes back to its old existence. It forever has a new standard of possibility. If you want to create the greatest art every created, you need some sense of what's possible, to get beyond all your personal ideas of the world, see farther, and explore new horizons.

It's the same with our own lives. To let go of our third-world attachments, we need something greater to hold on to, something sweet, stable, and glorious to base our lives on. We need the capacity, like an artist, to think beyond our current circumstances and results, to imagine possibilities. But our minds are filled with cares and concerns, many of which contain unknown outcomes and anxiety-provoking possibilities. We have relationships to attend to, children to care for, and bills to pay.

It's so easy to get trapped, caught in the place where we're just trying to get through the day, put out the fires… but when the blaze dies down, worries gather about tomorrow like paying the rent and the money we haven't set aside for retirement. There's no time for visualizing extraordinary things, eliminating hurry, or finding solitude and space to dream. That's all too intangible and non-transactionable. There must be results—some progress towards better circumstances and outcomes. But if success ever comes, it's always temporary, never fulfilling. So, we spend our days chasing lower-level-loves, consuming distractions like Pac-Man, gobbling up posts and reels, tasty meals, or Amazon's prime deals. We get more attached each day.

Thus, we need an expanded vision. One with clear visuals of long-term, never-ending beauties, unobscured by temporary setbacks and stressful situations. We need a solution, some way to solve this caught up in the urgent but surface-level life. There needs to be a new sense of determination, some joy-filled beauty that cuts sharp, like a knife, shaking us out of our busy, put-out-the fires lives.

We need to let go of our past—the limitations and attachments—so we can grasp what's possible. We're attached to our results and circumstances because we're afraid we might lose them, and when you're attached to something and you lose it, you go with it. You lose yourself. And nobody wants to be lost.

So how can we get on the right path, detach from our results and circumstances, and attach to God's peace and power? We need to catch a glimpse of the vast richness and depth of his love and beauty and unlimited possibilities that comes when we stop clinging to the story we've created about ourselves.

We need to trade our fears and lower-level attachments for his love, wisdom, and courage. Surrender all our attachments so we can connect deeply and powerfully to the creator of the universe. Surrender, then, becomes rather than a gesture of weakness, the most powerful act one can ever do. It's giving up your fears and mistake-prone self for the power that laid the foundations of the earth and holds the stars in place.

The gap between an anxiety-filled, self-in-the-center life and a life of deep contentment, joy, and confidence is surrender. You're never going to experience immense beauty holding on to your past and lower-level loves. You have to let go of the unstable ground beneath you to experience the freedom that awaits you.

Humility (an accurate view of self) and gratitude are crucial for surrendering your limited life in exchange for unlimited love, wisdom, and courage.

Three ideas to help you be more humble and grateful

1. You're either grateful or entitled.

2. Everything is here to teach you and help you; it's all working for your good.

3. You have no needs.

Grateful or entitled

For most of us, being immersed in the third world, we become attached to all those beautiful and wonderful things we can see, touch, and feel: possessions, achievements, looks, money, and status. When we're attached to those things we lose our freedom and creativity. Our vision becomes extremely short-sighted. Attached to what we want (or don't want) but can't control, we have anxiety.

We have too many thoughts from too many concerns because we're trying to control too many things. When we feel we know how things should be, and we see that they aren't that way, that's when we become anxious.

Anxiety and entitlement are generally closely linked. You can think of entitlement as "I should have things" or "I should be treated a certain way." It's the default, natural way to see the world.

Gratitude, however, is a powerful energy that doesn't co-exist with anxiety. It's an awareness of the truth about who you are and who God is. It's the opposite of entitlement, which is a lack of awareness. You're either grateful for your life or you feel like you've gotten shortchanged somehow, one of the two.

Here's a simple way to know if you're entitled: Ask yourself, "Have I been grateful for my life the last few days?" If you can't specifically say yes, "Yes I have," then you've been entitled. There's no in-between. Every day you're becoming either more grateful or more entitled.

The problem with entitlement is it's a fear-based attachment to your identity or comfort or any aspect of your life that comes from a limited, inaccurate perspective. Gratitude, on the other hand, sees clearly what you've been given, connecting you to inner peace and inner strength.

When you realize who God is and who you are, you're naturally grateful and humble. Humility paves the way for surrender. When you surrender your life's goals and dreams, fears and concerns to God, you walk in love. When I say "walk in love," I mean your energy is vibrating at the most powerful level there is, connected to God. If you're walking in fear, your energy is vibrating at a very low level, attracting negative energy.

You're either walking in fear or love, one or the other. You're either living in self-protection and entitlement (fear) or selfless expression and gratitude (love). When you walk in love you gain creativity to express that love because it produces joy. When you walk in fear you have more needs and live in reaction mode, because there's always threats to what's yours (your identity or family or some part of your life).

How to increase your gratitude (and see more beauty)

At the end of each day, spend a few minutes going through your day and look for all the gifts God gave you (ideally share your grateful moments with a partner). Look for specific moments in the day, the smaller the better. The subconscious likes clear pictures, and recalling specific moments trains your subconscious to see more each day.

Here's a few examples:

- When you got cut off in traffic by a reckless driver, you recognize that God may have just saved your life.
- When someone asks for help, you realize that God gave you the gift of being his hands and feet.
- When you have a moment or two without anxiety (or pain or anything else you don't want), you see that gift from God.
- When you realize that God gave you some challenge to overcome so you could learn and grow, you can be thankful for that opportunity.

So how can we consistently walk in love, not fear, and stay grateful, not entitled? Remember this foundational principle as you go about your day:

Everything is here to teach me and help me—it's all working for my good.

The truth is, God works all things for the good for those who believe in him. Sure, there's evil in the world, and bad things happen. But, and this is crucial, some things we think are bad are actually the best thing for us, and we rarely know when that is. And in the end, it's all going to work out for the good.

One of the primary reasons this principle is so important is because the best possible life is a life walking with God in the flow of resonance. That is, the amazing life that awaits you is a life of peace and joy, unattached to the ups and downs of your daily life (that's all God's responsibility—you're responsible for your heart and your actions—to believe and obey). It's a life of curiosity and adventure, one foot in joy and one foot in suffering.

To grow spiritually is to know God intimately. To know his love so deeply, and therefore his joy, so you have the self-control to be grateful and obedient in each moment, happy to serve and not be served.

Until you know at your core who God is, you won't know who you are, and until you know who you are, you won't let go of your endless busyness, striving to protect and secure all the ways you identify yourself. After all, if somehow you lost your job and possessions and achievements—all those markers in your life that need to be known—who would you be?

In the busyness of protecting our identities we're often too pre-occupied with getting things done to realize that what we ultimately want has already been done for us. It is finished.

The beginning of wisdom is to have awe and wonder for the grandness of God and his infinite love. If God's not real to you, if you don't occasionally have that *fall-on-your-knees-tears-streaming-down* type of experience now and then, it may be that you've been pre-occupied by urgent but non- essential tasks. If so, there may be too much noise to hear his voice. When you know God's love, you'll be able to share in the suffering so you can share in the glory.

Here's another principle that will help you be grateful and un-entitled:

I have no needs.

Everything you need, you have right now. If you don't have it, you don't need it. The idea for this principle came from a sign on the wall of a monastery:

> Dear monastery guests,
> If there's anything you need, please let us know. We'll show you how to get along without it.

The best life is a simple life, you and your purpose, training for heart transformation. Getting rid of what's not you is crucial. We need less thoughts from less concerns—so we can focus on the only thing we truly need—God himself. When you realize that what you think you need—better results, an easier life, more money—all those third world things, are really only preferences, and... God has already given you everything you need to live the Best Possible Life, you can start to let go of all your attachments and have the freedom you've always dreamed of.

The with-God life is a life of selfless sacrifice, giving up your strength for God's strength, transforming your desires for his. It's a life with few needs, sometimes repeated as a mantra: *I have no needs.* This is especially helpful to repeat when you're anxious or afraid to remind yourself that there's nothing that you need right now that you don't already have. To have no needs—to be un-needy—is to have an undivided heart; to walk by faith, not by sight, to walk in love, not fear, Truth, not transactions.

Victor Frankl, Nazi death camp survivor, said, "Everything can be taken from a man but one thing: the last of the human freedoms—to choose one's attitude in any given set of circumstances, to choose one's own way."

Like Frankl, in each moment, you have the choice. Will you be grateful or entitled? Will you walk in love or fear? The choice is yours.

How to Live in the Flow of Resonance

The object isn't to make art, it's to be in that wonderful state that makes art inevitable.
— Robert Henri, American painter

Once upon a time there was a farmer who lived outside a small village. He lived a simple life, a life of creativity and resonance. The farmer had a son who tended the crops and a horse that the son rode to plow the fields.

One day the horse ran away. The neighbors heard about it and said to the farmer: "We heard your horse ran away. What are you going to do? This is terrible news. How will your son plow the fields? Will you lose the farm?"

The farmer replied, "I don't know if it's good or bad, we'll see." The neighbors shook their heads at the poor farmer who couldn't see how terrible this was.

Several days later the horse returned—with another horse. It had met a wild horse when it was away, and so he now had two horses. The neighbors heard about it and said to the farmer, "We heard your horse came back and brought with it another horse. This is amazing! Now you can plow the fields in half the time!"

The farmer replied, "I don't know if it's good or bad, we'll see." The neighbors shook their heads at the poor farmer who couldn't see how great this was. The farm was saved—and now he could make a lot more money!

Several days later the farmer's son was riding the new horse to tame it and it bucked him off and he broke his leg. Guess who heard about it? Yup, the neighbors. They said, "Oh my gosh, this is the worst thing ever! How will you plow the fields? Will you lose the farm??"

The farmer replied, "I don't know if it's good or bad, we'll see." The neighbors shook their head at the farmer who couldn't see how bad this was.

Several days later a war broke out and the village took every able-bodied young man to fight, and many lost their lives. But because he had the broken leg, he didn't go to war and didn't die. Guess who heard?

Yeah, the neighbors. They said, "This is so incredible, the timing of your son's broken leg. He didn't have to go to war and so his injury likely saved his life and the farm as well!" What did the farmer say? "I don't know if it's good or bad, we'll see..."

We're like the neighbors.

Most of us spend our lives living transactionally, judging our results and circumstances and reacting emotionally—even though God works all things for the good (for those who love him). Somehow we've managed to live our entire lives in reaction mode, continually judging our results and circumstances negatively when we rarely know how things will turn out in the end. (Note: When I use the verb judge, I mean to lay down a negative verdict on self, circumstances, or others, without having all the information, which we almost never do. See Glossary).

Extraordinary people who live with deep contentment, joy, and confidence, live lives of creativity; lives of creation rather than reaction. They're creative because they don't judge their circumstances or themselves, God, or others. It's one of the primary ways to stay in the flow with God, resonating with him: develop non-judgmental awareness, and eliminate judgment from your life.

Perhaps the biggest difference between those who live extraordinary lives and those who do not is this: The Best Possible Life people, when difficult challenges arise, they see possibilities where everyone else sees problems. They believe their daily energy, rhythm, and connection to God is far more important than any circumstance.

They see possibilities because they've developed the ability to be non-judgmental. They have a broader vision—a higher awareness—than others because they're continually working on it. They regularly pull themselves (mentally and emotionally) out of their life in the third world and focus on the first world/realities of heaven. Every day they find moments to let go of all that's temporary and connect with what's eternal. They frequently remind themselves that everything is here to teach them and help them, that God is working all things for their good. So when the doubts, negative thoughts, and judgment comes, they're ready.

The Best Possible Life people prioritize the person they're becoming over the results they're getting. Because as you become the type of person who's non-judgmental and creative rather than reactive, you become someone who does great things—or just as powerful—does small things with great love.

So how do we decrease our self-in-the-center lives and increase our non-judgmental awareness? How do we mindfully (see the Glossary for a definition of *mindfulness*) let situations and thoughts come and go without being attached to them?

It all starts with selflessness. But selflessness is not possible without something beyond self to replace it—something far greater and more powerful, beautiful, and lasting. This is where God comes in. When you give your life to him, and as you grow in your apprenticeship to him, he'll reveal beauties to you that you've never imagined.

One of the things we can do—part of our two percent—is keep in front of our mind the principle that all things are here to teach us and help us, it's all working for our good. When difficult situations arise and concern and fear comes with it, remember the principle.

One of the major challenges we face in developing non-judgmental awareness is judging others. If someone is saying or acting in a way that's unwanted or unhelpful, you might consider the following principle. At first, you may completely reject it, especially when you think of the most difficult person in your life. For some of you, however, this principle will be life-changing. It goes like this:

Everyone does the best they can with what they have in their heart.

There's two parts to this principle:

1. Your heart is the control center of your life. Everything you think, say, and do is generated from the center of your being, your heart/spirit/will. Your heart, working with your

subconscious mind, runs your life. In your heart lies your greatest fears and biggest dreams, as well as all your beliefs, wounds, and traumas.

2. Everyone is always doing their best with the resources available to them. This doesn't excuse bad behavior, it simply explains it. When laws are broken (unless the laws are themselves unjust as St. Augustine and Dr. King taught us), there should be just consequences. What this principle says is that the human heart, like the laws of nature, acts according to the resources available to it.

Whenever someone (including yourself) acts in a way that's harsh or hurtful, it's because they lack resources such as love, joy, and peace, looking through a self-centered lens of fear or pain. We all lack those resources at one time or another, and so we all act in ways or say things that are not wise or helpful.

Imagine a young bully punches someone in the stomach for what looks like no reason. What I'm saying is that there is a reason, and when you understand this principle it will reduce your judgment, increase your compassion, and improve your ability to stay in the flow of resonance.

The bully, being human, has a deep need (like the rest of us) that's fundamental to his being: the need for unconditional love. It's the primary drive we all have and the deepest need of the human heart—to love and be loved, to connect deeply with others. When we're deprived of that love, we'll do anything we can to get it, even though we may not know that's what we're doing.

The greatest emptiness in life is the lack of love and connection, and the greatest punishment is the deprivation of human connection (like solitary confinement in prison, for example). When we lose connection or lack human touch for an extended period of time, we'll resort to most anything to get it. Even violence.

When this need for unconditional love goes unmet for months on end, or even years on end, that person will act out in some manner to get that love. Perhaps punching someone in the stomach for no reason. According to what was in the bully's heart: his background, his childhood, his fears, his wounds, his voids, his beliefs—it was the best he could do. It was all he could see to do. Filled with fear, his only resource was to lash out in self-protection.

Not only was it the best he could do in that moment, but *you would also have done the same thing* if you had the exact same fears, beliefs, wounds, and lens for seeing the world as he did.

This in no way excuses bad behavior, it simply helps you understand the wounded person behind the behavior and the broken world we live in. It allows you to step off the judge's bench and into the seat of compassion, connecting you with the person who's doing the best they can with what they have.

When you encounter someone making poor decisions, the only wise response is compassion for their lack of resources, and gratitude that you were given those resources. From there you can discern how to love them best.

One thing we learn from this principle is that no matter how hard we try, we can never do enough to be good enough. We're all flawed and in desperate need. We're imprisoned in our own hearts and can never get the joy and glory we're created for on our own.

To be loved, with no conditions to receive that love, is the greatest gift one could ever acquire. Amazingly, it's not only our deepest need, but it's also a free gift from God, the one who knows you intimately and completely. He knew when you would be born, when you would read this book, and when you would die. He knows every hair that falls from your head and every star by name.

This principle—**Everyone always does the best they can with what they have in their heart**—is helpful to observe in all aspects of everyday life, not just misbehavior.

Imagine playing chess against Norwegian grandmaster Magnus Carlson. Unless you're also a grandmaster, you're not playing the same game as Magnus. When he looks at the board, he sees a completely different board than you do. He sees dozens of moves, and along with each move, the potential outcomes for each. The rest of us see just a few moves, and they're likely not in the top two or three best options. We see two completely different worlds.

Any grandmaster chess player watching me play chess, in fact, would likely question every move I make (knowing there's far better moves). But he doesn't say anything, except to encourage me. No judgment. Why? He knows I'm doing the best I can with what I have.

Thus the grandmaster, rather than scolding me for the inferior decisions and poor choices, would encourage me. He knows that if he had my level of understanding and way of seeing the world, he would have made the same ignorant moves that I made.

Why this principle is so important

Most people live, as Thoreau said, lives of quiet desperation, constantly trying to be good enough or approved enough. But it's *never* enough. We've all been caught up in our own (third world) results and circumstances, pre-occupied with self and all the fears and limitations that go with it. In this naturally human lifestyle with self at the center, judgment is never far away.

When we judge, we generate negative energy that takes us out of the flow of resonance and away from an extraordinary life full of love, joy, and peace. Judgment of any kind takes us out of our flow of resonance and away from an extraordinary life.

We're all doing the best we can, at all times, in all walks of life. It's just that sometimes it's not very good (or even really bad). Whatever the situation, the amount of love, joy, and peace we have in our hearts directly correlates to the decisions we make and results we get.

When God sees you, he doesn't look at your performance or results, he looks at your heart. He knows that what's in your heart—who you are—is going to determine the course of your life. What he longs for is to fill your heart with the fearless love that he has until it overflows. That way, just by being near others, they'll feel a stirring in their heart, perhaps even a sense of the joy that awaits to fill their deepest need.

How to Pray

> *Prayer is the only entryway into genuine self-knowledge. It is also the main way we experience deep change—the reordering of our loves. Prayer is how God gives us so many of the unimaginable things he has for us. Indeed, prayer makes it safe for God to give us many of the things we most desire. It is the way we know God, the way we finally treat God as God. Prayer is simply the key to everything we need to do and be in life.*
>
> – Tim Keller, *Prayer*

Imagine you were invited to design your ideal vacation day, with unlimited resources—no constraints. How would you spend your day? Obviously you'd wake up and play a strategy board game while having some great food followed by amazing coffee. Likely next you'd get a massage to loosen you up before a round of golf, perhaps stopping at nine holes so you can do some fly-fishing, with your dog quietly watching in excitement beside you.

Before the sun sets—in a glorious, amber hug—you might squeeze in a game or two of pickleball before dinner and more board games. The setting would be filled with incredible wildlife along with amazing views and scents that capture your senses. There'd be the most serene lake with a solitary loon faintly beckoning you to come enjoy the tranquility. Likely you'd have those you love with you, and you'd be so excited, laughing and playing. Some version of that, right?

This paradise-for-the-day scenario is a glimpse of the human heart: it's built with a deep longing for joy. The problem is that our minds are far too limited to imagine anything more than happy moments—great feelings from amazing but fleeting circumstances.

When God gets hold of your heart, however, your imagination transforms. When new possibilities and beauties are introduced to your life your world is forever expanded.

Prayer is the entryway to another world—the first world—a world limited only by imagination and belief. It's the beam of sunshine that illuminates who God is and who you are, what he's doing in the world and how you can join in. It's the pathway to re-arrange your heart, so your lesser desires get enriched and expanded... so your heart grows into one that lives to glorify God and enjoy him forever.

Prayer isn't merely asking God for things (and maybe getting a dream vacation), it's developing a relationship with the creator of the universe, exchanging your fears for his love. It's uniting with the one who loves you more than you've ever been loved, who has greater plans for you than you've ever dreamed, and who can do far more than you can ask or imagine.

Primarily, it's making space for him to transform your heart, into one that's selfless and therefore fearless, one that dreams dreams as big as his.

Prayer is where your limited mind takes off its blinders and sees glimpses of the realities of heaven, the unlimited possibilities inherent in God's plans. It's the pipeline to wisdom, creativity, and beauty.

Prayer is the adoration and joy that comes from spending time with the one who loves you most. As author John Mark Comer puts it, "Prayer... that is... being with Jesus, is our primary portal to joy. It's the best part not just of each day, but of life. Prayer, of any kind, will always remain a chore, another task on the religious to-do list, until we come to realize that Jesus himself is our exceedingly great reward."

Prayer is sharing your journal with God—or perhaps better said—it *is* your journal to God—a sacred space to express the deepest part of your soul, your feelings and fears, longings and letdowns. The difference is, in this journal, God uses your pain and vulnerability to transform your heart.

When you pray, you're acknowledging your trivial pursuits and self-protecting heart... your extremely limited vision... and how you yearn to see what he sees, to know what he knows, and to love what he loves.

It's helpful to remember that you don't know what's best for you (third-world-wise—that is, your results and circumstances). But... God does. God always gives you, as Tim Keller says, what you would have prayed for had you known what he knows.

Here's what you might say:

Dear Father,

Thank you for the peace and joy that you've come to share with me, and all the gifts you've given me my entire life. Please strengthen me in my inner being, so that I can be rooted and grounded in love, so that I might comprehend who you are, what you're doing in the world, and how I can join in.

Transform my heart so I can grasp the width and length, height and depth of your love, so that I might know your love that far surpasses knowledge, so my fears get replaced with your peace.

Forgive me for the countless times I've tried to take your place and control what I cannot. Free me from self-reliance, pride, and indifference... from all the moments I've subtly demanded that my needs get met, especially for the majority of times when they were just preferences.

I don't know what's best for me and my family, Father, but you do. Your ways are so much higher than my ways. Help me let go of my self-centered blinders that block the views of all your extraordinary plans for me.

Bring into my life the teachers and disciples who can lead me towards you. Connect me with the ones who know your heart and obey your commands. Show me how to love sacrificially—especially the widow and immigrant, orphan and imprisoned, poor and impoverished—and radiate your grace. Lead me to the richest experience of your presence in my life, filled with all that you are.

I don't know how to do that father; that's why I deeply need you. I don't know you very well but you know the depths of my heart. You know my biggest fears and greatest dreams. You know my greatest mistakes and biggest failures and yet you still love me. You know every hair that falls from my head and all the ways I've tried to live without you.

Teach me how to let go of my life, so that every day there's less of me and more of you. Transform my heart so that when people see me, they feel your peace and joy, and when I'm squeezed, your love comes out.

I want to believe Father, help my unbelief.

In Jesus name,
Amen

So how do you connect with someone who loves you so much, there's nothing you could say or do that would change how much they love you?

Well, you let down your walls of self-protection and self-reliance. You give up your efforts to control what you can't control and you surrender all of it—your hopes and dreams, fears and failures—and offer it all to God.

To connect deeply with someone, you need time together, apart from the world. The power of prayer is most available when you step away from the noise, comparisons, and compulsions of the third world we live in. Then you can drop your guard and leave behind the self-protection, self-reliance, and indifference that's so limiting.

When you make room for the King of Glory—when you open the gates—you're opening your heart for God to fill the emptiness that only he can fill.

Prayer replaces a cluttered mind filled with anxious thoughts and limiting beliefs with a still mind, filled with God's peace and joy that goes beyond comprehension.

Here's How You Might Start Your Day (I've heard it's a decent option)

When you wake up, you might begin by pointing to heaven and say, "Father, I belong to you." Then as you start your day, turn on your morning music playlist... the one where all the songs relate to your purpose... then listen to the words of songs like "Live like that" by the Sidewalk Prophets and "Just be Held" by Casting Crowns.

Then you might face the sun (or a light that mimics the sun) and set the timer for ten minutes... a sacred boundary to soak up God's love... then turn on the worship playlist, just listening, no requests, letting your heart be transformed in gentle surrender. Ten minutes to orient your heart to the gifts you've been given, the Truth of who God is and where he is right now, and what he's prepared for you.

Next you might get out your bible, your journal, your work playlist (music you listen to while working or studying), your pencil, and perhaps essential oils. Once you have these things laid out, anoint your wrist with the oil, rub it on the other wrist, and say a little prayer like this:

Dear God,

Thank you for blessing me with this time to hear from you.

Please fill me with your spirit and all your love, wisdom, and courage.

In Jesus name,
Amen.

Then you might open your *Daily Walk Bible* (I'll send you a copy if you want one) and go to the current day's reading. Underline whatever stands out to you and if you have questions, go to the website biblehub.com and click on Strong's NASB in the upper right drop-down menu to see the original meanings of the words.

The bible is your official textbook for getting to know who God is, who you are, what he's doing in the world, and how you can join in. The more you absorb his words, the more you'll recognize his voice.

How to Manage Your Anxious Thoughts

In the bible there's a story of Jesus visiting two sisters, Mary and Martha. Mary sat at his feet while Martha (who's house it was) was distracted with all the preparations that had to be made. Martha, the hard working, busy homeowner, working for God himself, started to feel resentful that she was doing all the work. Jesus told her, however, that Mary was doing the better thing.

So Mary, the one not getting anything done, who set aside all the chores and busyness and important things to do, was doing the better thing than the one busy working for God? How does that work? That doesn't seem right… until you realize that God wants your heart more than your achievements. He wants your attention more than your sacrifice. Heart transformation—the person you're becoming—is the center point of this life, not your accomplishments.

Mary realized that God is the one in charge of her life and the direction it takes and results she gets. She created space in her life and made time to listen to God's words.

Anxiety is a mind with too many thoughts from too many concerns. In general it comes from trying to control what you can't control, as well as a lack of trust. When we're attached to what we want (or think we should have) but can't control, we get anxious. That attachment creates a busyness that turns into a harried life, full of hurry and anxiety. Anxiety comes from a heart that feels responsible for running the world, your world. Peace comes from being like Mary, prioritizing time listening to God over every other thing, even all the good things, even over doing God's work.

Learn to Navigate the Tension

The number one goal every day is to learn and grow—to have a heart a little more like Christ's—more love, wisdom, and courage. For this, we need challenges, obstacles, and difficulties. We need things to pray for. With problems comes tension—this is good. We need the tension so we can learn and grow.

When young trees encounter wind, they release a growth hormone called auxin that helps them stay grounded, grow taller, and heal wounds faster. It's the same with us. We need to be tossed in the wind a few times to stimulate the growth hormone—and learn to let go of self-reliance.

The problem we face is what to do with the tension or conflict when it comes so it doesn't turn into stress and anxiety. Stress and anxiety comes from trying to control what we cannot. This comes from a lack of trust, which comes from a lack of belief.

So when the storms come we can learn and grow by doing a couple things:

1. Look for the anxious moments and scary feelings rather than trying to avoid them. Embrace the tension—those moments when the future is uncertain and you have many things coming at that you can't control. Don't resist it or try to run from it. Lean into it—it's for your good; growth is coming. Visualize these moments ahead of time and see them for what they are: moments to help you learn to be okay with discomfort and times when things don't feel right... so you can grow.

2. Stop trying to control what you cannot. That's the cause of the anxiety and stress. You don't know what's best for you. Only God knows—and he might be the one *causing* the storm so you can grow. If you've prayed for faith for example (it's really the only thing that matters—expressing itself in love), well, then be prepared for God to answer your prayer by putting you in situations where you need it.

3. Ask yourself if you're willing to have these very uncomfortable feelings and live with them without resisting them.

4. In the discomfort and tension, ask yourself: "What do I want more, to get what I want in this moment, or to learn and grow and get better at these moments?"

Growth happens as you learn to trust God by embracing the tension and discomfort and not resisting it. To become someone you've never been, you have to be willing to face and embrace feelings you've never been willing to face—and release the outcome. God can transform your heart—and your whole life—but you have to be willing to let him tear out your old heart and build you a new one.

How to Make Big Decisions

When you have a big decision to make, here's an exercise that might help:

1. Get out your notepad (I like to use a big yellow one) or journal.
2. Turn on the worship music.
3. Listen.
4. Soak up God's love.
5. Thank him for all he's done for you.
6. If any ideas come, write them down.

Note that there's no aspect of trying to figure it out (in this exercise), or even asking God for the answer. He already knows your situation, what you need, and what's best for you. Praise, gratitude, and listening are a powerful trio to hear God's voice.

To make the best decisions, we need wisdom, and to have wisdom, we need time, space, and clarity to hear God's voice—without the chatter of outside noise and our own minds chiming in.

To pray is to expand what you believe is possible, to spend less time in our heads in self-reliance, and more time adoring, connecting with, and releasing everything to the one who created you, your family, your job, your life.

As you spend more time getting to know the God of the Universe, your heart will transform. You'll dream less of momentary happiness and paradise-for-a-day scenarios, and more of the infinite beauty in the good works that God prepared in advance for you to do.

In your solitary moments, the most beautiful day you can imagine will be one where you connect with God—in any setting. Often, it will be just sitting at his feet. Your greatest dream will not be a life filled with all the wonderful things God can give you, but a life filled with God himself. Because when you get God, you get everything.

How to Know if You're Doing God's Will

To know who you are is to know what you've given yourself to, what controls you, and what you most fundamentally trust.

— Tim Keller, *The Prodigal Prophet*

Imagine a honeybee living her life, but she doesn't know that she's part of a larger story, with particular duties and a specific mission (process the nectar, feed the queen, make the honey...). Her life wouldn't make sense if she didn't know her purpose. She'd just be dancing around, shaking her little bee-hind, trying to generate some buzz, not knowing that there's a grand story she's missing out on.

Without the connections, community, and single-minded devotion to a purpose beyond herself, she'd soon succumb to distraction or despair with all the challenges in life. She'd see the other busy bees and think that having a sweet job and being busy as a bee was all there was to life.

That would be a fatal mistake, and yet so many of us have made it. In Western culture we've measured our lives by the work we've done (or haven't done), because we don't know how to measure our hearts.

The key to knowing if you're doing God's will is to examine your heart—more specifically, to see what it worships, what it trusts in—what it believes. Is your heart grounded in faith, expressing itself in love—displayed in humility and compassion? Or have your beliefs reflected self-reliance, displayed by busyness and worry, striving to justify your existence?

Consider how you spend your days. Whether you sell real estate or really great cakes, whether you're the maid or the master, the key is *why* you're doing it. Because that will inform everything else about your day. Perhaps you think, "I work hard to feed my family and to serve God and do his will."

That's great, but there's much more to the Christian life (just ask Martha). You might be doing amazing things… volunteering at church, planting trees, sponsoring kids in Zimbabwe, buying girl scout cookies, giving 50% of your income to charity, and spending all your free time with your family. That's awesome, but it doesn't mean you're in right-relationship to God.

Doing God's will (and obeying his commands) is part of the bigger picture of being in right-relationship (that is, righteous) with God. As you study God's words, you'll see the word righteousness quite a bit. Two thousand years ago, the religious leaders closely monitored the religious laws and watched for those who didn't: they were self-righteous. Then Jesus came and said that our righteousness must surpass that of these religious leaders. How was that possible? Didn't those leaders follow all the rules and laws to a T? Perhaps they did—but they still weren't righteous in God's eyes.

Acts of kindness and charity and living a life of integrity are important—and a sign of where your heart's at—but it's only half the equation. You could donate all your money to the poor, work 15 hours a day as a missionary, and still be drifting away from God.

Righteousness, as Darrell Johnson says, means to be right-related. To be righteous—to be right-related—is to be in right relationship with God: to be surrendered to him and actively seeking to learn and grow to be like him every day. When you're in right-relationship with God, then all your other relationships—with yourself, your work, and all the people in your life—fall into place.

To be in right-relationship with God is to have a heart that obeys his commands AND has surrendered control of your life. Of course, surrender is not the human default. It's something to be done every day, sometimes every hour. When you're in right-relationship with God, you can fully relax because you're not the one responsible for your life—you're not in charge.

So how do you know if you've surrendered control? If you're doing all the right things, perhaps way more "good" than most Christians, isn't that the surrendered life?

Well... if you go to church, does that make you a Christian? If you spend all day caring for the poor, does *that* make you a Christian? While those are great things, they don't make you a Christian, and they definitely don't make you an apprentice. Those are good things, but good things can become distracting things, especially in a culture where numbers and accomplishments are highly revered. While humans look at appearances and achievements, God looks at the heart.

Here are a few questions to journal on, to see where your heart is:

1. What do you think about most?
   What you think about most reveals what's most in your heart, and likely, what you love most.

2. What do you worry about most?
   What are you most afraid of? What has regularly made you anxious? If you want to get to someone's heart, you have only to find out what they love most and fear most.

3. What gives you a sense of worth?
   As a professional athlete, my worth came from my status—how I compared to others. I felt good about myself when I performed well, but ashamed when I didn't. If your value comes from anything other than the value God placed on you when he died for you, you'll only be as stable as whatever that thing is.

4. What happens when you're squeezed?
   When unexpected, unwanted things occur, when life is out of control and painful things are happening, how do you respond? What's your immediate response to adversity? If the worst happens—like what happened to Job—do you reject God and go your own way? Or do you love God for who he is and not simply for what he can give you?

5. How offendable, embarrassable, and irritable are you?
   Our need for love is so deep, if we're not actively embracing God's love, we'll try to get our worth from what we achieve or how we compare. When we do so, pride and self-centeredness move us towards self-protection, self-promo-

tion, and indifference. We become easily offended, embarrassed, and irritated.

Consider this extraordinary example from Tim Keller about a heart that has freedom and joy, untethered to status or any sort of third world success:

Imagine you were the architect of the greatest cathedral in the world, and everyone knew it to be the best, and yet you didn't get credit. Could you be just as grateful and happy that it was built if someone else got the credit? Keller goes on: "Wouldn't you like to be the ice skater who wins the silver medal and yet is thrilled about those three triple-jumps the gold medalist did? To love it the way you love a sunrise? Just to love the fact that it was done? For it not to matter whether it was their success or your success?"

Your heart (spirit) is the part of you that will live forever. And thus the state of your heart—the person you're becoming—is the most important thing about you. The purpose of life on earth is to train your heart, for this life, and the one to come.

The first goal of training is to recognize, with all your heart, what God has done for you—to believe he is who he says he is, and that you are who he says you are. When that happens, your thoughts, words, and actions become more and more like his. Then you can become like him.

The Christian Deceptions

You might recall from chapter six that the two great deceptions in life are to think happiness is what you really want, and that if you're a good person, you should receive good things.

The two great deceptions in the Christian life are similar:

1. If you become a Christian and give your life to God, he should bless you with good things, or at least a life without suffering.
2. If your life is going great, and you're going to church, reading your bible, and obeying his commands, then you're in right-relationship with God.

The truth is, Jesus was perfect, and yet he suffered terribly. Job (from the bible) was a righteous man (right-related to God) and yet all his kids tragically died in one day, a day in which he lost his house and farm and all his livestock as well. None of this was his fault or had anything to do with his behavior or relationship to God. God was teaching Job to love God for God himself, not for what he could give him (as well as teaching millions of others for thousands of years).

If your life is going great and you're obeying his commands (the best you know how), that doesn't mean you're in right-relationship with God. God may have given you great skills, and maybe you're using them to do great things (even sharing the gospel) but at the same time you may be drifting away from God's heart. By the same token, if all ten of your kids died today and you lost everything you own, that doesn't mean you did anything wrong or that God is punishing you in any way (just ask Job).

So how do we know if we're doing God's will and walking with him if we can't tell by our circumstances or feelings?

Here are two areas to check and see if you're doing God's will:

1. Obedience
2. Apprenticeship

The Commands (obedience)

The two main commandments God gave us are to love God and love our neighbors as ourselves. There's many others, but they all fall under those two. If you do those two, God will transform your heart so you can do the rest (do not fear, love your enemies, etc.)—and give you the desire to do it. When God grabs hold of your heart, your greatest desire is to do his will, because that brings you the most peace, the most joy, and the most freedom. (Note: To love your neighbor as yourself is to recognize that God created you, your neighbor, and your enemies; and so you're to love and respect all human life equally, as well as yourself. This includes not being so self-centered that you don't feel God can forgive you or that you don't deserve his love.)

These two commandments are not things we "have" to do; they're laws embedded into the nature of the universe that are essential to living the best possible life. Obey these laws and your control center (your heart), will thrive; disobey and your inner strength and peace will dissipate. Cling to your life and lose it, give up your life and gain it.

So how do we love God and love others?

The Bible says God's children will be known by their love, and at the end of our lives, the justice we do and love we share will be measured in five ways:

1. Did you give food and drink to the poor?
2. Did you invite the poor into your home?
3. Did you give clothing to the poor?
4. Did you take care of the sick?
5. Did you visit the prisoner?

As a God of justice, God is extremely concerned with the heartbroken and disadvantaged. When we love our enemies and take care of the most needy and vulnerable, we're joining God in his work, connecting with his peace and power.

Doing justice doesn't get you into heaven, but it helps align your heart with his. And when your heart is aligned with the creator of the universe, he promises to come alive in your heart and lead your steps.

Apprenticeship: Surrender, Study, and Practice

Many of us who identify as Christians have focused on the savior part of Christianity (it's my favorite part actually) and hesitated over the Lord part (surrendering full control—my not-favorite). I guess surrendering control hasn't been my favorite because it's so scary. What if he asks me to give up my goals and dreams, or my home, or all my plans?

Most of my life I've preferred about a 90% surrender. That's been the sweet (and sour) spot I lingered at for too many years. Imagine being married and telling your spouse that you're 90% committed to them. That it's only one in ten days that you're with someone else. It's silly to think about. Marriage is all or nothing. When it's not, when you only go 90%, you're cheating yourself out of a life of peace and joy (not to mention your spouse). The problem is, the last 10% is the hardest.

Over the years however, I've realized, through lots of painful experiences, that Jim running Jim's life has not been the best life. It's so stressful! What God has told me over and over is to stop trying to control everything. Stop hurrying. Stop worrying. Let go and let God.

A God-surrendered life is very different than a Jim-running-the-show life. When I'm running the show, I'm responsible for my family and finances, friends and romance (or lack of), and the success of my clients. It's an attached-to-results life that creates anxiety and stress, guilt and shame. The God-surrendered life is one where my only responsibilities are my heart and my effort (not my results).

The rest is up to God; whatever I don't have, I don't need. Whatever I've done that didn't measure up or that I may feel guilty or shameful for, God is ready to forgive me—I just have to admit my weakness and accept his love and forgiveness each day.

In the Best Possible Life, my effort (my responsibility) is spent in apprenticeship. An apprentice, as you may recall from Chapter Eight, is a student learning by practical experience under an expert. The expert is God himself, Jesus—the one who came to earth to love you and show you how to love.

Apprenticeship starts with surrender, then immediately moves into study and practice.

A big part of the surrendered life is to realize that you'll often have no idea what he's up to, and so many times you'll disagree with what you think he's done or at least allowed. This last part is important, because if you would run the universe exactly like him, then you would be as wise as him. But since he's infinitely wiser, of course you're not likely going to agree with a lot of what he does or allows. This is the whole idea of surrender.

What I've preferred to do is obey and adhere to the commands that I found reasonable. Perhaps we can call it a good-guy version of Christianity. Be a good person, love others, ask for forgiveness when I make mistakes. It's a luke-warm Christianity, neither hot nor cold. Do the right things and give 10 percent of my income to the poor, but protect the other 90%, as Josh Garrells says, "with my guns." When I live this way, I've created my own religion. The gospel according to Jimbo. I don't recommend it unless you want to have a near mental breakdown in Denver.

When things happen that I disagree with or don't understand (and there's a lot), and I still submit to his authority, that's when God transforms my heart the most—with more love, wisdom, and courage. Perhaps in those tough times where God seems distant, I'm a bit like Thomas Merton. He had no idea where he was going, couldn't see the road ahead of him, and couldn't know for certain where it would end. But even though he felt lost, he trusted God. We're so used to be led around by our feelings, and yet feelings can lead us to make terrible decisions.

When your heart has been surrendered such that your greatest desire is for God himself, however, not what he can give you, then your life will unfold with indescribable beauties amidst all the setbacks of life. While you'll still have all the normal life challenges living in a broken world (jobs comes and go, markets crash, people die, etc.), you'll have a depth of peace and joy that you've never experienced.

Here's some key characteristics of a heart that's surrendered to God:

- It's extremely aware of the deep debt we owe God and our complete inability to redeem ourselves.

- It has immense humility and gratitude, along with great sorrow for all the evil and suffering in the world—and most of all, for our own sin.

- It continually seeks to increase in self-awareness and gentleness and decrease in self-reliance and the indifference it creates.

- It's a heart that hungers and thirsts—like a deer pants for water—to be in right-relationship with God.

- It's an undivided heart, founded on right-relatedness and gratitude, and revealed by love and tangible service to the poor and marginalized, as well as support for human rights around the world.

- It's filled with tenderness, compassion, and joy.

- It takes risks to make peace, perhaps at great cost to self; willingly sacrifices its own desires and security for the sake of being right-related with God, self, and others.

Grow in Grace

The surrendered, with-God life, the best possible one, is the life of the beloved—the one who's most deeply loved. In other words, when you give your life to God, you're set to receive immense, unconditional, and endless love from the creator of the universe—as his precious treasure. As you grow in your knowledge of God, you'll grow in your understanding of his unmerited gifts and stop trying to be good enough to deserve it. You'll get out of the courtroom—continually on trial for all your actions—and into his loving arms.

The more time you spend with God, seeking to know him and be with him, the more you'll know it's him you want most and the more he'll transform your heart. You'll realize that all your striving and worries came from a caught-up-in-the-third-world-life, busy trying to control what you cannot and trying to get what you don't need.

You'll grow in faith and it will show in your humility and compassion because you won't have to spend any more energy searching for love and acceptance, trying to justify your existence. As you grow in faith you'll see God's love transforming your heart in nine areas: love, joy, peace, patience, kindness, goodness, faithfulness, gentleness, and self-control.

These nine characteristics of a transformed heart will lift your spirits and help you live the spirit-led, with-God life, unattached to the distractions and compulsions of the third world. This in turn will prompt you to share undeserved gifts with others, remembering that they're doing the best they can with what they have in their hearts. Your life becomes one endless (sometimes bumpy) journey, daily discovering God's grace—his love and joy, kindness and compassion—and sharing it with the world.

Conclusion

You were created for an extraordinary life. An infinite supply of love, wisdom, and courage is waiting to empower you. All you have to do to start this journey is open your heart and let go of your old life and the fears and limitations you've clung to.

Your life is a story, and a question, literally, of life and death. The life you're meant to live can be a scary path to take, because it means the death of your old self, the one you clung to, the one with its tired attachments and fears. The scary path is also the one that's gently and patiently calling you, right here, right now.

The world desperately needs you. Even if you're reading this on April 1st, it's no joke. There's a great need in the world, and *you* are what the world needs. Your true self that is, the one created by God, for God, aligned with God. No one in the world can do what you can do. No one has your background, your experiences, and your heart. No one has the precise plans laid out for them by God that you have. The question of life and death is asked of you every day: Will you give up your fears and self-absorbed past—the one we all have? Because when you do, you give the world hope, and we all need hope.

What I'm asking you to do is let go of your past—all the fears and wounds and self-protection—and let the King of Glory come

CONCLUSION

into your heart and run your life. It starts with accepting his invitation—he's inviting you right now to let him into your heart, to live a life beyond anything you've ever imagined. Will you let him in?

If you accept his invitation, it's the greatest decision you'll ever make. You should know by now, however, that—like anything of incredible value—the cost is high. The life he's invited you to is not a one-time decision. It's the decision to become an apprentice—for life. To become a disciplined learner and surrender your life, study God's words, and devote each day to becoming like Jesus himself: filled with his love, joy, peace, patience, kindness, goodness, faithfulness, gentleness, and self-control.

Surrendering your life to God means letting go of what you've fiercely held on to, the things that once made up your identity, and grabbing on to God instead. It's putting your faith, trust, and hope in what holds the heavens in place—eternally powerful and stable, but invisible to the eyes. It's accepting a peace and joy you didn't know existed, in a faith-filled, unknown future.

Rather than a weakness, surrender is the most powerful thing you can do. It's like having some drinks and surrenduring the car keys—by far the wisest choice. We've all been intoxicated, deceived into clinging to the fears and attachments that drag us down. Self-reliance, so crucial as a child, has moved us into self-protection and self-promotion, which has become pride, fear, and indifference.

Our self-in-the-center lives cost us connection and compassion, dissipating our power and separating us from every good thing. In that life, we grew to love most what we experienced with our physical senses, causing us to miss out on unseen, unimaginable beauties.

What you love most is what's running your life. Whatever that thing or person or pursuit is, that thing you think about and worry about most, that's what you're worshipping. That's your god. You're as stable as it is.

With the Best Possible Life, your greatest goal changes from getting more for yourself, to sacrificing yourself—for God, and others. You join a community of people learning how to be selfless and therefore fearless, in pursuit of a heart filled with outrageous, unconditional love. We're in this together, on an adventure with God taking us places we've never dreamed.

Because we're human, we all have our own flaws and weaknesses, so we encourage each other without judgment... meeting everyone where they're at in the journey. We know they're doing the best they can with what they have in their hearts—and we know that if we had their heart and their resources, we would do the same.

Remembering this, we continually seek humility so we can have an accurate view of self, so we can see more broadly, learn more readily, and connect (with God, self, others, and work) more easily.

Then we can be courageous and believe.

This life is an expedition, with many ups and downs. It's the pursuit of an undivided heart, one where God most readily uses the humble and the weak, not the strong ones at their peak.

When you start this journey, it's easy to think that if you do all the right things, God will bless you with good things, third world blessings. It's tempting to think that if you're a good person, you should be happy. But you'll realize that happiness and comfort and getting your desires met could be the worst thing for you. And so you pray, and trust, that God will change your heart to be more like his, to love what he loves. You pray that your desires

CONCLUSION

will transform, from mostly asking God to change your circumstances, to mostly asking God to change your heart.

Your daily practice becomes training your heart, because everything you do flows from it. You'll pray for a re-ordering of your loves—so what you love most becomes what's most empowering. Rather than spending the alone moments in your life dreaming of better results and circumstances, you'll dream of loving others outrageously, especially the poor and marginalized, the widow and the orphan, the refugee and the prisoner. I know that since you've read this far, God has already started training you.

The ultimate power, to have an undivided heart, not only transforms your desires but changes the narrative that is your life—your whole story changes. Rather than being the one running the show, you give up control of your life and give it to God.

It's a complete restructuring of your day-to-day life. The great obstacles to the spirit-led, surrendered life—busyness and hurry, are deconstructed. You become unhurried. Since you're no longer relying on yourself, you no longer need to rush around trying to get things done or shore up your sense of security or future. Sunday (or whatever day you choose to put the work down and soak up God's love) might even become your favorite day.

Your highest goal switches from third world success to first world beauties—heart transformation. Of course you still set goals and pursue dreams, but now your greatest goal is to get know Jesus, to have a heart like his.

As you grow, your heart will long for what God's heart longs for: to free those who are wrongly imprisoned, to lighten the burden of others, to let the oppressed go free, to feed the hungry, to shelter the homeless, and to clothe those who need it.

In your life as a Christian apprentice, your love and service to others—especially those who cannot pay you back—will bring you freedom and joy, setting you free from comparison and envy.

You'll still have fear, and sometimes anxiety, but now you know that the best possible life has one foot in joy and one foot in suffering. This allows you to embrace the pain of a broken world with the power of a God who created the universe. You'll be intentional about compassion (suffering with), and you'll schedule time to join in the suffering, placing yourself next to the poor and disregarded.

You'll no longer be attached to all the situations in your life: work and home, finances and family, as well as all your relationships. You'll know that every situation you encounter, every person you meet is here to teach you and help you—it's all working for your good. You'll realize that your job is to not judge the situations in your life. Your job—your life's work—is to believe.

It takes courage to believe, that despite all the wrongs in the world, God is who he says he is, and despite all your failures, you are who he says you are. When you take courage, God will give you the ability to love him and love your neighbor, to do justice, to love kindness and to walk humbly. When you live like this, every good thing—every single thing you need—will be added to you.

As you go forward and pray for a transformed heart, remember that you'll grow in your proportion to your willingness to let go of your self-absorption and the fears that go with it, so you can connect with God's infinitely loving and fearless self. Then you can get busy living the life, growing spiritually—knowing God's love, accepting his love, and sharing his love.

Becoming a Christian means becoming an apprentice. This does not reduce your suffering, but it does transform it. When

CONCLUSION

you surrender your life to God, you have meaning in the suffering (to become like Jesus and have his love, joy, and peace). You have hope in the realities of heaven that awaits. You not only embrace the tough times, you also pursue doing hard things to learn not to be a slave to comfort or your feelings and desires.

The Best Possible Life is unveiled in the pursuit of self-mastery, but truth be told, true mastery can only be fully developed through daily surrender to the Master, the King of the Universe. God gives his love and resources to people who don't deserve it, and the ones he's empowered the most are not the talented ones, but the ones who've recognized their weakness. The extraordinary life does not come from strength or toughness, it comes from surrender.

So let's not boast of our strength, but of our weakness, because when we are weakest, his light shines the strongest, revealing his path for you. It's a path that changed the world, 2,000 years ago and continues today. Step by step you'll join the saints who've gone before you and the angels singing with you, all helping you realize... in this moment, you are infinite.

PS.

When I was going through the lowest point in my life, a few months after meeting Zoe, the homeless harpist, I had this dream...

I was in a rowboat, rowing hard with sweat pouring off my forehead. And I was getting nowhere. I looked down and saw a massive rope (perhaps three to four inches thick) tied around my waist. I looked behind me and saw that it was taut, going up at a 45-degree angle tied to an ocean liner! No wonder I wasn't going anywhere.

Then I saw—standing at the helm behind the steering wheel—Jesus. The original Zoe! He said, "Jim, whenever you're ready, jump on in."

So... what about you? You ready? Ready to let go of your anxiety and self-striving and hand over the steering wheel? It's so scary to let go of the wheel, to give up control. But, of course, it's the best decision you could ever make. It's giving up your rowboat for the ocean liner. It's all waiting for you—your calling. *The Best. Possible. Life.*

PS.

Let's connect!

If this book was meaningful to you, please help us share it with others by reviewing it on Amazon.com. Your review could be what prompts someone to read the book, which may change their life--and their family's life.

I'd also love to hear personally from you as well. Email me at jim@innerexcellence.com and let me know how this book impacted you. Be sure to sign up for my newsletter/blog at www.innerexcellence.com/newsletter and follow me on Instagram @innerexcellencejimmurphy.

FAQs

1. **How can an all-powerful, all-loving God allow horrible evil and suffering?** God's heart is broken because of all the suffering and evil in the world. When he created humans, he gave us free will to choose him or reject him (otherwise it would not be love). So when Adam and Eve chose to use their freedom to reject his will, they became separated from God. Pain, suffering, and terrible evil came into the world. God was so heart-broken that he sent his only son to die in our place, to conquer evil and death.

2. **Don't all major religions basically teach the same thing/ lead to the same place?** There are many similarities to many of the major religions: take care of the poor, pray to God, love others, etc. But there is only one major religion, Christianity, that says being a good person will do nothing to save your life. Christianity is the only religion that offers a personal relationship with the Creator of the universe, based on nothing you've ever done or could do, a completely free gift.

3. **Isn't Christianity and religion in general a crutch, a fantasy of faith that goes against science?** Everybody on earth has an immense degree of faith about things we don't know, just

to survive. We can only hope that other drivers will not cross the center line and crash into us and end our lives, for example. Since nobody was around thousands or billions of years ago when earth was formed, we're all guessing as to how it all started. Science is great at explaining repeatable phenomena in the natural world, but terrible at explaining unseen things like love and fear and desire. It takes just as much faith to believe the earth and humans and all the incredible intricacies that make up the universe was all random as it does to believe there was a creator behind it all.

4. **I'm spiritual but not religious. Everybody has their own truth and so do I. What's wrong with that?** This sort of faith or religion, that everything is relative (I've got my truth and you've got your truth) goes against the idea of moral absolutes. In other words, if you can create your own religion (believe what you want), then what's wrong with rape and torture? A person could believe that that's ok (perhaps like natural selection/survival of the fittest) and you'd have to allow them to believe that. This means you couldn't condemn them if they practiced what they believed.

Most people, however, do not believe that rape and torture are morally ok. This means that there needs to be moral absolutes beyond our own personal beliefs.

5. **Can't I just be a good person?** Yes, you can and I certainly hope you are. But you could be Mother Theresa's hero and role model and sacrifice your entire life for the poor, but you would still not have any more to offer God to get into heaven than a murderer or thief. No amount of good you could possibly do would be enough to gain the infinite paradise and

perfect goodness that is heaven. It's a free gift from God, one that cannot be earned, it must be accepted—with a repentant heart that acknowledges your sin and self-centeredness.

6. **How do you reconcile all the violence in the Bible?** The Old Testament is filled with violence, you're right. Before Jesus came, there seemed to be sort of an evolutionary law: survival of the fittest. Then Jesus came (as told in the New Testament) and completely changed everything. Life went from killing your enemy to loving them.

7. **What about contradictions in the Bible?** When Jesus came, he changed the world. Out with the old law, in with the new law (Christ himself). Jesus often shared stories with metaphors that weren't literal (hate your mother and father; I have not come to bring peace but a sword, etc.). The Bible was written several thousand years ago and so understanding the culture and language at the time is important to understand the text.

8. **What if I give my heart to God but am indifferent to the poor or haven't really helped them much?** Perhaps your heart hasn't yet grasped the heart of God, or you've been too busy, or something has grabbed your attention away from this crucial part of God's heart.

9. **What if I give my heart to God, spend all my spare time doing charity work, but lack humility and compassion?** Doing charity work is an incredible gift to the world and directly connects to God's broken heart for his children. But if you don't have selfless, sacrificial love for others, especially those who disagree with you (even your enemies), and for those of lower status than you, then you gain nothing.

10. **If I give my life to God, promising to love him with all my heart, can I still be a professional athlete or business leader and aspire to become the best in the world?** God has given each of us unique gifts, some of which are extraordinary skills of athleticism or leadership. Even if you're the #1 ranked golfer in the world, your greatest gift isn't hitting a golf ball; it's the realization that you were created by God and for God, to love him and others, and that any skill you have was given to you by God.

Once you realize that, I do think you can have extremely high goals that take immense dedication and long hours, and still love God with your whole heart and love your neighbor as yourself. (I'm a performance coach after all, paid to help athletes and leaders achieve extraordinary success).

The hardest part is thinking you're somebody special because God gave you that gift. The spiritual life's two greatest challenges may loom larger for you than others: self-absorption and self-reliance.

It's important for athletes to realize that there's no inherent meaning in golf or tennis, football or baseball on their own (no more than ping-pong or board games—as great as those are). Their value is teaching you to how to love your opponent (your partner in the dance), put others first, and train your heart, mind, and body for a life of resonance.

The meaning is in what you're pursuing (heart transformation) while you train, learning and growing how to love God and love others more than yourself. Even though those are just games, since you're being paid to do them, it's important to work as if unto God himself, doing everything and treating everyone with respect and honor.

While I think you can have a million dollars in the bank and still be a Christian, are you really loving your neighbor as yourself if you have two jackets and he has none? Even if you gave 1,000 jackets away, and now have two, and your neighbor has none, aren't you back to square one? This is not a judgment, just a question (perhaps more for myself than anyone).

11. **If I become a Christian, would I have to give up all the fun?** My life has been one long obsession about maximizing everything, going for the most fun, trying to get the most from each moment. What happens as you get older, you realize that if you just go for maximum pleasure, you'll eat all the chocolate in the house, max out your credit cards and end up sick and broke. You'll learn that if you have big dreams, you've got to sacrifice temporary pleasures for long-term growth or you'll never get anywhere. You'll also learn that what you want even more than maximizing temporary happiness is to maximize your life in every way, which means developing inner strength, inner peace, and the fearlessness that comes from selflessness that leads to the best possible life.

When you say fun, I'm assuming you mean playing strategy board games (of course) or going camping or fishing (big-time) or playing golf (oh yeah). In my experience, all those amazing things you love get enhanced, not diminished when you invite God into your heart. Now you can finally relax and play for fun and not worry or feel self-conscious about what others think, or stress about your life—because God's running your life and you're not.

12. **Which political party is the Christian one?** Well, there won't be any Republicans in heaven, that's for sure. Of course there won't be any Democrats or Catholics or Pentecostals or any other group either. There will be a party though.

The politics of Jesus were completely opposite of the politics of the world. He came to earth as the true ruler, the divine king, and yet he displayed his authority not by controlling and commanding others, but by laying down his life for others. Heaven, our true home, doesn't have political parties. It's often by forgetting their true home that Christians get so aligned with a particular political party that their politics takes over and becomes their religion.

You'll know if politics has become your religion when you lack love, grace, and humility with those who believe different than you. When your passion about your rights or public policies overtakes your compassion for your neighbor (like the person you're talking with) and it's become more important than your own heart transformation, then your politics has become your god.

Remember, the enemy is evil itself (not a person or groups of people), and the violence and hatred evil brings. The enemy doesn't care what you believe, just that you keep hating and fighting. The most important evil to be aware of is the violence and judgment in our own hearts. The greatest solution to evil is the love we share, not the policies we believe in. Eventually every knee will bow to the God of the universe—he will make it happen, not you.

If you feel called to get involved in the political process or even debate about it, the Christian approach is to let sacrificial, outrageous, unconditional love for your enemies (and those you disagree with) be your defining feature.

One of the greatest attachments people have is attachment to their opinions, to being right, especially to their political views. When you become a Christian, however, much more important than convincing someone to adopt your view, is to share God's love with them by being a great listener. If they're convinced you love them, then they can experience God.

13. **If a pastor or preacher is performing miracles, speaking the truth, and his church is growing, does that mean he's a disciple of Jesus?** Actually, no. God can speak through anyone and use anyone to do miracles as he often has. A better way to know if a spiritual leader is a disciple of Jesus is their fruit: Are they humble and compassionate? Are they peacemakers? Do they love their enemies? Are they an advocate for the refugee and immigrant, widow and orphan, imprisoned and poor? When they're squeezed, does love come out?

It's super easy to fall into the trap to think if my results and circumstances are being blessed and I'm doing "God's work," then I'm going in the right direction (for you or a pastor). The reality is that some preachers and well-known religious leaders—when they come face to face with God—God will say, *I never knew you.* While their actions may have been great, their heart was disconnected from God. The heart is the key.

14. **What's the minimum needed to get into heaven in case someone wants to maximize their time on earth and still**

get eternal paradise (asking for a friend)? That's like asking the minimum needed to graduate from high school or college—yes there is a minimum but it's the wrong question. It's like asking if there's a way to be last in medical school and still be a doctor. A much better question is, how can I have the best possible life right now and experience heaven on earth many times over before I get there?

Please note: These are deep philosophical questions that cannot be completely answered in a paragraph. See *Where to go from Here* for more resources.

Where to Go From Here

Read these books

Life of the Beloved: Spiritual Living in a Secular World. Henri Nouwen. 2002.

This short book has been my most gifted book besides my own over the last 20 years. Nouwen is one of the most gifted thinkers/writers I've ever read and this work on the spiritual life is powerful, concise, and easily read.

The Freedom of Self-Forgetfulness: The Path to True Christian Joy. Tim Keller. 2012.

This very small book is kind of the Christian handbook for performing with *Inner Excellence*.

Practicing the Way: Be with Jesus. Become like him. Do as he did. John Mark Comer. 2024.

So many great teachings on how to live out the best possible life.

Daring to Live on the Edge: The Adventure of Faith and Finances. Loren Cunningham. 1992.

Cunningham (YWAM founder) reminds us that God in 2024 is the same God that parts the Red Sea, turns water into wine, makes the blind see and the lame walk, and is doing countless miracles every day.

The Insanity of God: A True Story of Faith Resurrected. Nik Ripken. 2016.

If listening to this book doesn't bring a sense of humility and urgency in your life to help those in need, then nothing will.

The Prodigal God: Recovering the Heart of the Christian Faith. Tim Keller. 2008.

Keller's book powerfully shares what the Christian life looks like and reveals the ever-so-common trap of judging others that comes from trying to be good.

Mere Christianity. C.S. Lewis. 1952.

Perhaps the greatest book ever written on Christianity. Although a longer book (written in England shortly after WWII), the writing is so down-to-earth and relatable.

The Dangerous Act of Worship: Living God's Call to Justice. Mark Labberton. 2012.

Labberton's book transformed the way I view worship. Now I see worship as a tight bond with righteousness (to be right-related) and justice (the "doing" part of life we're called to live).

The Beatitudes: Living in Sync with the Reign of God. Darrell Johnson. 2021.

Darrell's book taught me about the beatitudes in a way I'd never heard; essentially that the eight beatitudes are eight characteristics of a heart that's been grabbed hold by God.

Daily Devotion

Jesus Calling. Sarah Young. 365 Day Devotional. 2015. You can also get the app (free).

The Daily Walk Bible NLT. 2013.
This Bible (I use New Living Translation) made it much easier to soak up God's words by giving me 15 minutes a day to engage with his wisdom. Note: if you know anyone (in the USA) who would like one, please email livedeep@innerexcellence.com with the name and mailing address.

The Listener's Bible, (New International Version) narrated by Max McLean. So powerful to get God's words into your heart through hearing—faith comes from hearing. McLean is amazing.

Find some role models (here's a few of mine)

Shane Claiborne
Shane moved into one of the poorest neighborhoods of Philadelphia to live with and serve the poor. He helped start a community called The Simple Way. Shane's an advocate for the homeless and an activist against violence, specifically the death penalty and gun violence in America. He wrote The Irresistible Revolution, which had a big impact on my life.

Loren Cunningham
Loren is the founder of Youth With a Mission (YWAM), a global outreach program run strictly by volunteers (they live off donations) which has expanded to every country in the

world. One of their ministries is called Homes of Hope (which the Inner Excellence Freedom Project has teamed up with).

David Wilkerson

David, author of *The Cross and the Switchblade*, did street ministry in New York City and shared God's love with some of the city's most notorious gang members.

Bryan Stevenson

Bryan is a Harvard-educated African-American lawyer and Christian in Alabama, who's dedicated his life to helping the poor, incarcerated, and condemned. Bryan is the founder of Equal Justice Initiative. Read how Micah 6:8 impacted Bryan's life. *Bryan Stevenson: Do Justice, Love Mercy, Walk Humbly* Nashville Christian Family. Cheryl Sloan Wray.

Brother Yun

Brother Yun (Liu Zhenying) is an exiled Chinese Christian house church leader who's been imprisoned and tortured for sharing the good news of God's love. You can read about his life in The Heavenly Man.

Check out these Podcasts

The Darrell Johnson Podcast
Timothy Keller Sermons Podcast (by Gospel in Life)
Practicing the Way Podcast
Crazy Love Podcast (Francis Chan)

Acknowledgments

The two greatest teachers of my life (outside my family) have been Dr. Timothy Keller, founding pastor of Redeemer Presbyterian Church in New York City, and Dr. Darrell Johnson, pastor/professor/teacher in Vancouver, Canada. If you see many ideas or words that resemble either of those teachers, well, it's because I've tried to become a disciplined learner of how they see the world and the realities of heaven. I'm so grateful God sent these extraordinary teachers into my life.

Thank you to my amazing book coaches and editors, James Carpenter and Meg Mittelstedt. Your insights and feedback have been invaluable. Thank you also to Michael Scott Williams for your editorial help.

There's been many other amazing teachers God has blessed me with, especially:

- Dr. Ken Shigematsu, Pastor of Tenth Avenue Alliance in Vancouver, Canada
- My spiritual director and great friend Pastor Nick Osborne (and Jamie Osborne), of Tofino, BC

A special thank you to my brother Patrick Murphy who introduced me to so many of the great teachers I've learned from; people like Dr. Dallas Willard, Dr. John Ortberg, and Dr. Greg

ACKNOWLEDGMENTS

Boyd, three teachers whose books and sermons have impacted me tremendously; Richard Lopez, University of Arizona, FCA Campus Director has also shared many wonderful things over the years; Pastor Jonathan Michael, who has been a wonderful resource of biblical knowledge for many years; Ricky Scruggs, who I've had many insightful discussions with including one that initiated the idea for the Three Worlds Model.

Thanks to all the early readers, especially a few who went above and beyond: Connie Geier, Marvin/Julia Hofer, Pat/Betty Murphy, Dr. PJ Murphy, and Titus Murphy.

Thank you Pat and Betty Murphy (Winnipeg, Canada) and Mike and Wendy Bishop (Vancouver, Canada) for your friendship and wonderful generosity offering your homes for me to have a special place to write.

Thank you to all my friends at James Valley Hutterite colony for all the visits and amazing food and fellowship you've shared with me the last few decades... and for helping me learn about Anabaptist life and experience Christian community.

Finally, thank you to my dad who devoted his life to studying God's commandments and showed me how to take care of those in need, and to my mom who's grace and gratitude, humility and discipline resembled the life of Jesus more than anyone I've ever met.

Note: While Tim Keller is now in heaven, that leaves Dr. Darrell Johnson as the sole living teacher who has had the greatest impact on my life (besides my family - no pressure Dr. J!). You can find him in Vancouver, BC, still sharing the gospel as a semi-retired pastor and professor, serving in part-time ways with Regent College (Teaching Fellow), Alpha Canada (as Bible teacher), and The Way Church (as part of the teaching team).

Notes

Best Possible Life: How to Live with Deep Contentment, Joy, and Confidence—No Matter What.
This subtitle comes from Dallas Willard when John Ortberg asked him what he needed to do to help his church experience greater levels of spiritual growth. Willard replied, "You must arrange your days so that you're experiencing deep contentment, joy, and confidence in your everyday life with God." John Ortberg. *Soul Keeping* (Grand Rapids: Zondervan, 2014).

The Merton Prayer
Thomas Merton, *Thoughts in Solitude.* (New York: Farrar, Straus, and Giroux, 1958).

My story
p. 3. In the Fall of 2003 I was invited by Ricky Scruggs (former roommate in pro baseball) to help him with the grand opening for Centerfield Baseball Academy in Tucson, Az. I decided to move there to the desert and help him part-time while I lived a life of relative solitude.

p. 5. Zoe is the Greek word for life. *I came to bring you life and life abundantly.* – Jesus Christ (John 10:10)

NOTES

Chapter 1

p. 18. Charles Cooley, American sociologist. August 17, 1864 – May 7, 1929.

p. 18. David Marchese, "David Byrne Isn't Himself," *The New York Times*. Dec. 9, 2023. https://www.nytimes.com/interactive/2023/12/10/magazine/david-byrne-interview.html

Chapter 2

p. 20. Jeff Goins (perhaps an atheist), shared a powerful quote.

p. 24. David Foster Wallace. *This is Water*. Kenyon College Commencement speech. 2005.

Chapter 3

p. 29. If you "free" a fish from water... "Modern people like to see freedom as the complete absence of any constraints. But think of a fish. Because a fish absorbs oxygen from water, not air, it is free only if it is restricted to water. If a fish is 'freed' from the river and put on the grass to explore, its freedom to move and soon even to live is destroyed. The fish is not more free, but less free, if it cannot honor the reality of its nature. The same is true with airplanes and birds. If they violate the laws of aerodynamics, they will crash into the ground. But if they follow them, they will ascend and soar. The same is true in many areas of life: Freedom is not so much the absence of restrictions as finding the right ones, those that fit with the realities of our own nature and those of the world." -Tim Keller, *Every Good Endeavor: Connecting Your Work to God's Work* (New York: Penguin Books, 2014)

p. 30. In order to hit the best shot... Teddy Scott, caddie to world #1 golfer Scottie Scheffler, personal correspondence. 2024.

p. 32. Dr. John Yates III is the father of early reader (of this book) Xander Yates and the Rector at Holy Trinity Anglican Church in Raleigh, NC. This quote came from his sermon titled, "Straight to the Heart" Jan. 29, 2024.

Chapter 4

p. 34. You were born to experience absolute fullness of life (in Greek: zoe), to do great things and feel fully alive. "For we are God's handiwork, created in Christ Jesus to do good works, which God prepared in advance for us to do." – Ephesians 2:10

p. 35 Tim Keller, *Prodigal God*, (New York: Penguin Books, 2011).

P. 35. He delights in every detail of your life. Psalm 37:23.

p. 36. He also created you to do amazing things—too many to list. Psalm 40:5. (NLT)

p. 36. ...which He prepared in advance for you to do. Ephesians 2:10.

Chapter 5

p. 37. The idea for the three worlds came from a discussion about mind, body, spirit with performance coach and counselor Ricky Scruggs.

p. 40. "Since you have been raised to new life with Christ, set your sights on the realities of heaven, where Christ sits in the place of honor at God's right hand." – Colossians 3:1
(see also p. 43, 92, 97, 113, 121, 146).

Chapter 6

p. 48. You were created for glory, but..."And since we are his children, we are his heirs. In fact, together with Christ we are heirs

NOTES

of God's glory. But if we are to share his glory, we must also share his suffering." Romans 8:17

p. 48. One foot in joy and one foot in suffering. I heard a podcast once from Fuller Seminary where the lady being interviewed said the best stories have one foot in hope and one foot in suffering. So good! I thought, *Yes! And the best lives have one foot in joy and one foot in suffering.* I can't seem to find that podcast or recall her name.

Chapter 7

p. 53. "'Now this was the sin of your sister Sodom: She and her daughters were arrogant, overfed and unconcerned; they did not help the poor and needy." Ezekiel 16:49-50.

p. 54. You may gain the whole world but lose your soul. Matthew 16:26.

p. 54. "Dunning-Kruger Effect," Wikipedia, updated October 9, 2024. https://en.wikipedia.org/wiki/Dunning%E2%80%93Kruger_effect

p. 56. Martin Luther King Jr. *Letter from Birmingham Jail*, 1963. King (1929-1968), was a Baptist minister and civil rights activist.

Chapter 8

p. 60. "Religion that God our Father accepts as pure and faultless is this: to look after orphans and widows in their distress and to keep oneself from being polluted by the world." – James 1:27

P. 60. "History of Atheism," Wikipedia, Updated October 10, 2024, https://en.wikipedia.org/wiki/History_of_atheism

P. 61. Easter: There are multiple theories on how to describe Jesus's death and resurrection. How it reconciled us with God

169

(e.g. atonement) and how it achieved victory over evil and death (e.g. Christus Victor). One view focuses on Christ taking punishment for our sins, while another focuses on defeating the devil.

p. 61. "And since we are his children, we are his heirs. In fact, together with Christ we are heirs of God's glory. But if we are to share his glory, we must also share his suffering." Romans 8:17

p. 62. As John Mark Comer, *Practicing the Way*, (New York: WaterBrook Publishing, 2024).

Chapter 9
p. 67. ...every good thing will be added to you. Matthew 6:33

p. 67. "If you cling to your life, you will lose it; but if you give up your life for me, you will find it." Matthew 10:39

p. 71. ...but instead, you walk by faith, not by sight. 2 Corinthians 5:7

Chapter 10
p. 73. The example of the light switch came from Tim Keller's sermon: *The Parable of the Pearl: On Priorities*. Timothy Keller Sermons Podcast by Gospel in Life.

p. 77. Tim Keller. Prodigal Prophet. (New York: Penquin, 2018).

Chapter 11
p. 80. *"Then they asked him, "What must we do to do the works God requires?" Jesus answered, "The work of God is this: to believe in the one he has sent."* John 6:29

p. 81. The primary resource is the Bible. There are many great translations. I generally read the New Living Translation (NLT),

NOTES

New International Version, (NIV), or New American Standard Bible (NASB).

p. 82. "Teacher, which is the greatest commandment in the Law?" Jesus replied: "'Love the Lord your God with all your heart and with all your soul and with all your mind.' This is the first and greatest commandment. And the second is like it: 'Love your neighbor as yourself." - Matthew 22:36-39

p. 82. "He has told you, O man, what is good, and what does the Lord require of you; to do justice, and to love kindness, and to walk humbly with your God." – Micah 6:8

p. 84. "When the Son of Man comes in his glory, and all the angels with him, he will sit on his glorious throne. All the nations will be gathered before him, and he will separate the people one from another as a shepherd separates the sheep from the goats. He will put the sheep on his right and the goats on his left. Then the King will say to those on his right, 'Come, you who are blessed by my Father; take your inheritance, the kingdom prepared for you since the creation of the world. For I was hungry and you gave me something to eat, I was thirsty and you gave me something to drink, I was a stranger and you invited me in, I needed clothes and you clothed me, I was sick and you looked after me, I was in prison and you came to visit me.' Then the righteous will answer him, 'Lord, when did we see you hungry and feed you, or thirsty and give you something to drink? When did we see you a stranger and invite you in, or needing clothes and clothe you? When did we see you sick or in prison and go to visit you?' The King will reply, 'Truly I tell you, whatever you did for one of the least of these brothers and sisters of mine, you did for me.' - Matthew 25: 31-40

p. 89. When you have inner peace... This idea came from a sermon Tim Keller preached (like most ideas in this book!) but I don't recall which one. If I say, "As Tim Keller says," in every paragraph, however, you may begin to think I'm crazy.

Chapter 12

p.94. Mark Leibovich, "Tom Brady Cannot Stop," The New York Times, 2015. https://www.nytimes.com/2015/02/01/magazine/tom-brady-cannot-stop.html

p. 95. (p.73) John Mark Comer, *Practicing the Way*, (New York: WaterBrook Publishing, 2024).

p. 95. St John of the Cross, *Dark Night of the Soul*, (New York: Dover Publications, 2012). This is a reference to the essay *Dark Night* by Spanish mystic St. John of the Cross (1542-1591). (Not Batman).

p. 101. "Do not conform to the pattern of this world, but be transformed by the renewing of your mind. Then you will be able to test and approve what God's will is—his good, pleasing and perfect will." – Romans 12:2

p. 102. John Ortberg, *The Life You've Always Wanted*, (Michigan: Zondervan, 2015). One day Dr. John Ortberg, a young pastor, asked his mentor, Dr. Dallas Willard, "What do I need to do to be spiritually healthy?" After a long pause, Dallas said, "You must ruthlessly eliminate hurry from your life."

Chapter 13

p. 105 Thomas Merton. Letter to a Young Activist. 1966. Reprinted in Dorothy Day's Catholic Worker newspaper in 1977. See it here: https://jimwallis.substack.com/p/thomas-mertons-words-of-hope-for

NOTES

p. 110. Everything is here to teach me and help me, it's all working for my good... This principle is based on Romans 8:28: "And we know that God causes everything to work together for the good of those who love God and are called according to his purpose for them."

p. 112. I read the monastery sign quote in a book but can't recall where. If you know, please contact us at livedeep@Innerexcellence.com.

Chapter 14
p. 119. Henry David Thoreau. *Walden*. (London: Pan Macmillan, 2016).

Chapter 15
p. 121. Tim Keller, Prayer, (New York: Penguin, 2014).

p. 123. John Mark Comer, *Practicing the Way*, (New York: WaterBrook Publishing, 2024).

p. 127. If you'd like a copy of the Daily Walk Bible and you live in the United States, send an email to livedeep@innerexcellence.com and we'll send you one.

p. 128. "Hormones and Tree Health: The Connection You Didn't Know About," Treenewal.com, 2023. https://treenewal.com/hormones-and-tree-health-the-connection-you-didnt-know-about/

p. 129. "The only thing that matters is faith, expressing itself in love." Galatians 5:6.

Chapter 16
p. 132. Tim Keller. Prodigal Prophet. (New York: Penquin, 2018).

p. 134. The definition of righteousness came from Dr. Darrell Johnson in his sermon *Alive in an Olympic-Sized Craving*, Jan. 31, 2010.

p. 135. Darrell Johnson gave a sermon with similar thought-provoking questions to gauge where your heart is: *No Other Gods Between Us*, Sept. 13, 2015

p. 136. Tim Keller, *The Freedom of Self-Forgetfulness*, (La Grange: 10Publishing, 2012).

p. 141. This list is adapted from the Beatitudes, Matthew 5:3-12.

[3] "Blessed are the poor in spirit,
for theirs is the kingdom of heaven.
[4] Blessed are those who mourn,
for they will be comforted.
[5] Blessed are the meek,
for they will inherit the earth.
[6] Blessed are those who hunger and thirst for righteousness,
for they will be filled.
[7] Blessed are the merciful,
for they will be shown mercy.
[8] Blessed are the pure in heart,
for they will see God.
[9] Blessed are the peacemakers,
for they will be called children of God.
[10] Blessed are those who are persecuted because of righteousness,
for theirs is the kingdom of heaven.
[11] "Blessed are you when people insult you, persecute you and falsely say all kinds of evil against you because of me.
[12] Rejoice and be glad, because great is your reward in heaven, for in the same way they persecuted the prophets who were before you."

NOTES

Conclusion

p. 145. "Whoever does not bear his own cross and come after me cannot be my disciple. For which of you, desiring to build a tower, does not first sit down and count the cost, whether he has enough to complete it." – Luke 14:27-28

p. 145. "But the fruit of the spirit is love, joy, peace, patience, kindness, goodness, faithfulness, gentleness, and self-control." – Galatians 5:22

p. 147. "Above all, guard your heart, for everything you do comes from it." – Proverbs 4:23

p.147. "Do you really think this will please the Lord? No, this is the kind of fasting I want: Free those who are wrongly imprisoned; lighten the burden of those who work for you. Let the oppressed go free, and remove the chains that bind people. Share your food with the hungry, and give shelter to the homeless. Give clothes to those who need them, and do not hide from relatives who need your help." – Isaiah 58:6-7

p. 148. "Jesus answered, 'The work of God is this: to believe in the one he has sent.'" - John 6:29

p. 148. "He has told you, mortal one, what is good; And what does the Lord require of you But to do justice, to love kindness, And to walk humbly with your God." - Micah 6:8

p. 149. "But he said to me, "My grace is sufficient for you, for my power is made perfect in weakness." Therefore I will boast all the more gladly about my weaknesses, in insults, in hardships, in persecutions, in difficulties. For when I am weak, then I am strong." – 2 Corinthians 12:9-10

Glossary

apprentice: a disciplined learner; one who studies under an expert in order to become like the expert. An apprentice of Jesus is someone who devotes their life to study, prayer, and practice—in order to live and love like Jesus lived and loved.

compassion: to suffer with. The love, wisdom, and courage that comes from humility; compassion interrupts our lives; you cannot be compassionate when you're busy or in a hurry; an extension of empathy (where you take off your shoes and step into another person's shoes) then taking the next step, walking—perhaps barefoot—with them in order to help them.

courage: to embrace the heart of God; to believe that God is who he says he is. The more courageous you are, the more love, peace, and joy you have. The greatest confidence is the courage to believe that God has got you no matter what (see faith).

discernment: to use wisdom to make decisions, especially as opposed to judgment; always seeking how to love others best; unconditional love may mean giving others what they don't want, or not giving them what they do want, or perhaps setting a boundary with them.

GLOSSARY

ego: The part of the mind that's always comparing, always threatened, and never satisfied; you're always on trial because everything you do is evaluated to see if you measure up—it never rests. The ego inflates and deflates your sense of self, creating a false self that can never fully relax.

empathy: to take on the perspective of another person and feel what they're feeling; the first step towards compassion.

faith: the assurance of things hoped for (divinely guaranteed), and the evidence of things not seen—the conviction of their reality; faith comprehends as fact what cannot be experienced by the physical senses.

glory: the brilliance and weightiness of infinite, inherent worth, for which you were created; the infinite universe and all the love, wisdom and courage contained in Glory Himself, the Creator of it all.

GPS: Gratitude. Presence. Showtime. This is a ten-minute tool from *Inner Excellence* where you set your timer for three minutes and then look back at your last 24-48 hours at all the gifts you've been given, and give thanks for them. After three minutes you do it again and focus on being present (and aware of who God is and therefore who you are). The third segment you set the timer for three minutes and visualize your goals and dreams. Finally, the last minute you finish with your arms in the air, raised towards heaven in a big Y, asking God to fill you with his love, wisdom and courage.

happiness: a positive, temporary feeling attached to a circumstance; good feelings based on good circumstances (what's happening). When circumstances are bad there is no happiness (although there may be forced smiles); happiness is always a by-product of circumstances (see joy).

humility: an accurate view of self; to be free from self-inflation or self-rejection; the product of a clear mind and understanding heart.

Note: A humble person knows that inner strength and fearlessness comes from selflessness. They also know that every good thing in their life is largely the direct or indirect result of things they had nothing to do with: the century they were born, their country, parents, coaches, friends…as well as their mind, heart, and physical health, the list is endless; a truly humble person is a very grateful person; humility and gratitude, wisdom and surrender are closely linked; they lead to joy and peace. A humble person knows that our days on earth are like grass; like wildflowers, we bloom and die. The wind blows and we are gone, as though we had never been here.

Inner Excellence Ultimate Dream Journal: The Inner Excellence version of Dr. James Pennebaker's therapeutic journaling. There's been over 400 scientific, peer-reviewed studies on his therapeutic journaling. It's pretty straightforward… writing for 15-30 minutes a day for four days straight on your greatest trauma or current concerns. Contact us at livedeep@innerexcellence.com and we'll send you the Inner Excellence Ultimate Dream Journal guide.

joy: a deep, pervasive sense of well-being, freedom and gratitude, independent of circumstance (deeper and broader than any pleasure); sense of delight that comes from awareness and anticipation of the beauty, grace and glory you were created for Note: Joy, the by-product of love, is the fundamental attribute that leads to all the other attributes of the best possible life: peace, patience, kindness, goodness (integrity), faithfulness, gentleness and self-control. Joy is possible when unhappy about the circumstances (see happiness), even in the midst of suffering—indeed it's the strength to get through suffering.

judge/judgmental: v. to lay down a (negative) verdict of someone, some thing, or yourself (even though we don't have all the information—though we often think we do); generally accompanied by negative emotion. The measure you use to judge others will be used to measure yourself; when you judge others, you are also judging yourself. When you judge, you're making two mistakes: One, you're lacking grace and wisdom when you judge and two, your vision narrows, losing out on creativity and solutions. See discernment.

mindfulness: a mental state of awareness of the present moment, unattached to the thoughts and feelings, impulses and compulsions that arise; acknowledging and accepting those things without judging them.

peace: deep contentment, awe and wonder; profound rest and harmony that comes from having relationships in their proper place (see righteousness); offspring of joy.

pride: self-conscious concern for self, or as Oxford scholar C.S. Lewis calls it, ruthless, sleepless, unsmiling concentration on the self. Self-absorption; leads to comparison and self-consciousness and the need to have more or be more than the next person. With pride there is constant calculation on how one is perceived. Pride is the great barrier to excellence because it is the biggest obstacle to learning from failure. Pride is concerned about perception because protection of the ego is its greatest concern, and the ego is only concerned with comparison (see ego). Since learning and growing is the greatest goal in the process of mind and heart transformation, pride is the great obstacle. A proud person can be easily angered or embarrassed whereas a truly humble person cannot be humiliated. Pride and bitterness go together because there is no bitterness without pride. Pride and fear go together; thus, self-protection and humiliation are always a concern (see humility).

resonance (or flow of resonance): the vibration of energy where your energy matches the natural frequency of your true self and God's love; when you have a clear mind and unburdened heart; a state of gratitude and joy, fully engaged, unattached to results and circumstances; the by-product of love, wisdom and courage.

righteousness: to be right-related (to have your relationships in the proper place and priority), especially the big four relationships: God, yourself, others, and your work; being right-related brings a clear mind and undivided heart, and most of all, joy and peace. (Note: the definition of right-relatedness came from Dr. Darrell Johnson in his sermon *Alive in an Olympic-Sized Craving* Jan. 31, 2010).

self-awareness: Consciousness of your thoughts, feelings, and actions and the ability to see them objectively, in order to grow. The ability to see your own beliefs, patterns of thinking, feeling, and behavior and how they affect your life and those around you. Self-awareness is the first step toward growth and zoe.

self-care: Controlling your energy in order to be your best self. Eating healthy, exercising regularly, loving others, visualizing, and getting centered are all examples of self-care.

self-centeredness: the default, limited viewpoint of seeing everything from how it affects you (and your family/world); fuels self-consciousness and the ego. With constant self-focus, your limits and failures continually emerge. A preoccupation with self that's attached to your past and sees life from a "What's in it for me?" point of view; the greatest limiter of the zoe life and biggest challenge we all face.

self-concern: The focus on self that leads to self-consciousness, doubt, anxiety, and eventually fear.

self-conscious: concern about what others think of you; the feeling of discomfort from being noticed and feeling judged by others.

selflessness: Putting the greater good and what's right before individual desires or needs; to continuously develop self while simultaneously forgetting about self.

self-inflation: an inaccurate view of self. Attributing any positive result or circumstance to the self (generally to feel better about yourself). See pride and humility.

self-mastery: The self-control and presence that come when your life is surrendered to the Master (Jesus). Self-mastery is focused on learning and growing in love, wisdom, and courage; the pursuit of self-awareness, self-discipline, and self-education in order to grow to be your true self. The journey toward zoe which supersedes external achievements or worldly success. Closely associated with mastering the ego in three ways: to become unembarrassable, unoffendable, and unirritable.

self-rejection: Personalization of failing to live up to some standard. Rather than objectively analyzing a setback or an unwanted outcome, it feels as if you not only failed in the task but also are a failure as a person; viewing self as less worthy because of some external event or opinion (see shame).

self-renunciation: to put honor, virtue and the well-being of others ahead of oneself. It's not self-rejection but rather selfless rejuvenation into a person of unconditional love. As Leo Tolstoy put it: "the whole world knows that virtue consists of the subjugation of one's passions, or in self-renunciation."

self-righteous: believing that your ideas and behaviors are morally superior to others.

sense of self: Your feeling of value; your sense of identity. If you have a strong sense of self, you're comfortable being uncomfortable, need no validation, are comfortable in your own skin, and don't rely strictly on successful outcomes to feel good as a person. A person with a weak sense of self lives in constant comparison with others and continually looks to satisfy the needs of the ego. Your true self only comes by surrendering your life (and ego) to the creator of the universe so you can be filled with His love, wisdom and courage.

GLOSSARY

shame: a lonely feeling that you're flawed, unworthy. Whereas guilt is tied to an event (I did something bad), shame is tied to a person (I am bad).

state: The combined status of your heart, mind and body at any given moment; how you feel overall—physically, mentally, emotionally and spiritually (see feelings).

subconscious mind: The part of the mind that works beyond your awareness, allowing you to function and not think of every little thing (such as tying your shoes, walking, and breathing). Immensely more powerful than the conscious mind, it's continually being programmed to make your habitual thoughts and beliefs reality. The subconscious and the heart work closely together.

surrender: Give up control of your life and; letting go of self-reliance and letting God take care of your needs, fears, and concerns; selflessness of unconditional love; trading in your little lollipop for the whole candy store.

wisdom: to know who God is and therefore who you are, what He's doing in the world, and how you can join in; keen insight on how to live with absolute fullness of life; an understanding heart; the expanded vision that sees unobstructed views of beauty, opportunities, and connections with others; closely related to (unconditional) love and courage; the greatest thing one could ever seek.

zoe: absolute fullness of life (God himself); the state of being possessed of vitality; life, real and genuine; vigor and vibrancy of life; the culmination of love, wisdom, and courage; self-actualization.

Made in United States
Troutdale, OR
01/12/2025